Creative Drama in the Elementary School

LANGUAGE ARTS SERIES

Paul C. Burns, Editor

UNIVERSITY OF TENNESSEE

**DIAGNOSTIC TEACHING
OF THE LANGUAGE ARTS**

Paul C. Burns

**LANGUAGE ARTS FOR THE EXCEPTIONAL:
THE GIFTED AND THE LINGUISTICALLY DIFFERENT**

Lester N. Knight

**CREATIVE DRAMA
IN THE ELEMENTARY SCHOOL**

Barbara M. McIntyre

CREATIVE DRAMA IN THE ELEMENTARY SCHOOL

BARBARA M. MCINTYRE
UNIVERSITY OF VICTORIA, BRITISH COLUMBIA

F. E. PEACOCK PUBLISHERS, INC.   ITASCA, ILLINOIS 60143

Contents

Foreword

THE LANGUAGE ARTS are the core of the elementary school program. They are a vital and central force in the living and learning of young people—providing the foundation for practically all classroom activities and serving to interrelate the many areas of the curriculum. Thus, quality teaching of the language arts is essential to the entire program of the school as well as crucial to each child's learning.

Most of the language arts textbooks used in teacher education treat the total spectrum of the language arts, and few supplementary materials are available. So this series of paperback books came to be because of the editor's conviction that certain topics of the elementary school language arts need to be explored in thoroughness and depth by authors with a particular competence and interest in the topics.

In writing the books, the authors have made every attempt to be practical and specific—yet open-ended. In this way, the series is appropriate for undergraduate elementary education students and the elementary school classroom teachers who want to design and implement an effective program of language arts for children. The books could also be used to good advantage by consultants and participants in workshops and other professional renewal projects for elementary school teachers.

Paul C. Burns, Editor
The University of Tennessee

Acknowledgments

THE WRITER gratefully acknowledges the cooperation and understanding of the many children, teachers, parents, and friends who appear anonymously in this book. It is their story that I pass on to encourage the teachers of today and tomorrow to make elementary school living come alive with dramatic experience.

To Katherine Turner, who typed the manuscript and kept everything in order at the same time, goes my special thanks. Without her patience and advice the publication date would not have been met.

Introduction

THIS PUBLICATION is one in a series of paperbacks concerned with elementary language arts. It is designed not for the drama specialist, but for classroom and student teachers with little or no experience in drama. The author believes that language arts is taught from the moment the first pupil arrives in the classroom until the moment the last pupil leaves. The teacher needs to continually add new methodological strings to her educational bow. Drama is one string which is frequently missing from her repertoire. To help her gain insight into the dramatic process and how this process can stimulate children's language learning is the purpose of the book.

The examples cited are not presented as models to be rigidly followed. Rather they are examples which hopefully may stir the imagination of the teacher and aid her in developing her own drama games and classroom activities.

Those references marked with an asterisk have a specific purpose. They are presented as a catalyst. They form a logical sequence of readings and research to aid the teacher who wishes to delve more fully into the art of drama and drama education.

Chapter 1

Educational Rationale
for Drama in Language Arts

"THE FIRST THING you've got to remember is that you must not talk."
"What will I do then?"
"You just sit and pay attention to the teacher."
"All day long?"
"Yes. Just do what she says. Don't talk to anyone or argue like you do at home. It's a bad thing to talk at school."
"I won't go."
"You have to go. You have to be quiet and learn how to read and write like the teacher says."

This is an accurate account of a conversation which was overheard one September morning as two small brothers prepared for the first day of school. The older of the two was to enter second grade and the younger was to enter kindergarten. In big brother fashion the seven-year-old was concerned that his five-year-old brother—so dynamic and talkative at home—get the proper orientation for the experience to come. From his two years at the school in question the seven-year-old knew what was important. Talking was out and doing what the teacher said about reading and writing was in. Oral language was an art to be used only by the teacher to tell the children what to do and not to do. Teachers would be horrified to learn that their pupils felt this way. Intellectually they know that they tend to talk too much. They know that just because they "teach," learning does not automatically happen. They probably agree with James Moffet (1968, p. 13) when he says that the two biggest misconceptions in the language arts are: (1) "that the learner must be given facts about our language system, concepts of literature, and advice about composition;" (2) "that language arts concerns reading." The majority would agree that the children need to use language continuously. They understand that oral language must precede both read and written language. They probably agree with the program concept expressed by John R. Linn et al. (1968, Teacher's Guide, p. vii) when he describes the philosophy of *Language Patterns* as follows:

> Language Patterns envisages language as a three-dimensional component of human personality. It is seen as (a) an instrument of communication (b) an instrument of logical reasoning . . . Language Patterns recognizes language as the symbolic representation of experience and views experience as falling into the following classifications: (1) basic sensory experience which Piaget considers vital to subsequent cognitive development; (2) social experience involving the interplay of the child and his peers in the group; (3) environmental experience in the community.

The translation of these theories into practice, however, is difficult, particularly for the inexperienced teacher. Workbook and standard pencil and paper activities are important. But, strict adherence to constant desk work with little or no opportunity for active sensory, social, and environmental experience frequently stifles the excitement of learning and leads to a hatred of school. In the search for methods to translate theory into action and stimulate positive learning, teachers need to develop active and interesting language activities. Helping the child learn about himself and his world through his senses, his place in society through actively communicating with his peers, and his community through interaction within an exciting learning environment, is an important purpose of the language arts.

James Moffet (1968, pp. 35–36) believes that drama or "acting out" is the starting place for the language arts from kindergarten through third grade. His purposes in "acting out" are:

1. To promote expression of all kinds, movement and speech harmonizing, and reinforcing each other
2. To limber body, mind, and tongue
3. To begin to single out the verbal mode from the others and thus to activate speech in particular
4. To forge drama into a learning instrument for continued use throughout all grades
5. To make the first school experience with language fun and meaningful in the child's terms
6. To habituate pupils to working out harmoniously in small groups
7. To further peer socialization of a learning sort not usually possible outside of school
8. To gain intuitive understanding of style as voice, role and stance, and of rhetoric as achieving effects on others
9. To develop in the more familiar mode of dramatic play those characteristics necessary for the less familiar process of discussing, such as attending, responding, interacting, and turn taking
10. To exercise and channel emotions.

Although there is little specific research data to support these wide purposes, the results of several studies conducted in the United States over the past twenty years lend substance to the idea that there is great value in "acting out" in the language arts. A series of studies on the effects of creative drama on the speech and personality of elementary children was conducted at the University of Pittsburgh. Ludwig (1955) showed that a group of kindergarten children who participated in a three-month program of creative drama made a significantly greater improvement in articulation than did a similar group who did not participate. McIntyre (1958) showed that a group of older elementary children significantly reduced their number of articulation errors during a six-week summer program of creative activities, which included a great deal of "acting out" experience. Irwin (1963) showed that there were measureable changes in the personal and social adjustment aspects of personality as measured by the California Test of Personality in a large group of third grade children who had experienced a twelve-week program emphasizing "acting out."

More recently Tucker (1971) conducted a study concerning the use of creative drama in primary reading readiness. She showed "that creative dramatics has an influence on developing the verbal skills of reading readiness beyond that of maturation and normal schooling. Specific abilities such as listening and vocabulary were developed."

Another study conducted at Illinois State University by Carlton and Moore (1968) showed how dramatization technique could be successfully utilized in elementary reading.

Eloise Hayes (1970), professor of education at the University of Hawaii has developed and tested some drama techniques in her language program with Hawaiian children whose progress in standard English was hampered by their use of "pigeon." The most extensive U.S. study in drama which can be directly related to language arts grew out of the work of one of the educational laboratories set up by the federal government in the late sixties. The Aesthetic Education Program, CEMREL, Inc., has developed an exten ive drama program. The Theatre Games File (1971) contains a ealth of research supported ideas for inexperienced and experienced teachers. These and many other studies conducted in the United States support the contention that drama has a positive effect on language learning.

Although substantial research evidence is lacking, subjective reports in professional journals and text books from both Canada and England also support the contention that drama should form an important part of the language arts program. *Nobody in the Cast* (Barton et al. 1969) includes excellent dramatic language activities for the older elementary child. Two other publications entitled *Creative Dance in the First Three Grades* (Boorman 1969) and *Creative Dance in Grades Four to Six* (Boorman 1971) contain a wealth of dance and movement ideas which relate directly to language arts. *A Different Drummer, An Ideas Book for Drama* (Kemp 1972) is also an excellent source for inspiration and material. These and other Canadian references add substantially to the available practical material for the classroom teacher.

The educational drama materials from England are more extensive and deal with drama as a subject and as a technique. The work of Dorothy Heathcote of the Institute of Education at the University of Newcastle is outstanding. Her writings (1967, p. 27) and films such as *Omnibus: Three Looms Waiting* provide excellent stimulation and encouragement to drama specialists and classroom teachers. The Dartmouth Seminar Papers (Barnes 1968) produced by the National Council of Teachers of English, which report on the English drama scene as it pertains to the teaching of English, are invaluable, as are other reports (Heathcote 1967). An extensive survey of drama in England conducted by Her Majesty's Government in 1967 is also exceedingly helpful (Education Survey 2). It is systematically organized to show not only what is being done in drama, but how it relates to all aspects of education. It contains loosely documented but specific references to the value of drama in the language arts. There is also a wide variety of English textbooks which deal with drama. *Development Through Drama* (Way 1967) appears to be the most useful for the teacher whose main interest is the teaching of language arts in the classroom.

These few studies, reports, and text books from a larger body of material from the English speaking world, although subjective in nature, lend effective support to the contention that creative drama can be an exciting and effective approach to language arts. It is, therefore, the purpose of this writer to help classroom teachers use creative drama to increase the child's understanding of himself through dramatic sense awareness and movement experiences, his ability to communicate with his peers through role playing and characterization activities, and his understanding of his community and its relationship to its problems through improvisation and dramatization. If the classroom teacher keeps these broad purposes in mind as she uses the dramatic process, the writer believes that the basic language skills of listening, speaking, reading, and writing may be more effectively and happily attained and used.

DEFINITION OF TERMS

1. Language arts are the tools used to communicate with others. Generally, they are listening, speaking, reading, and writing. These four skills should not be considered as separate subjects to be taught. They are communication skills linked under a common ability known as language. To this list can be added the skill of playing or acting out. This fifth skill is the binding thread throughout the language arts.
2. Children's drama is an all encompassing term for a group of activities involving the dramatic process with and for children.

    1. Creative drama is the informal facet of children's drama. It includes the spontaneous dramatic play of small children, the guided dramatic play of older children, and the improvisational games, characterizations, and dramatizations which arise from the child's interactions with his environment. It is not scripted or performed for an audience.
    2. Children's theater is a scripted performance for an audience of children. It may be performed by children for other children or for adults (as in the presentation of a school play for parents), but more generally it is theater performed by adults with the purpose of entertaining a child audience.

3. Drama education is a part of the educational program in a few school districts. It exists within the curriculum as does music education, art education, and physical education. It is conducted as a separate subject with a content to be understood and skills to be learned and practiced.
4. Drama in the language arts is used within the language arts as a technique instead of as a separate subject. The drama skills are identified and used as a means of furthering all language learning. There is a process to be understood and broad language goals to be attained.

Chapter 2

The Dramatic Process

COMMUNICATION is the center of the educative system. Language, oral and written, is one of the chief means of communication. Too often communication in the elementary classroom is a one-way process—the teacher sends and the child receives. Communication should be a circular process, with the teacher and the children all being receivers and senders. When a classroom environment conducive to this circular communication is created, vital learning can take place for all concerned. The children learn to communicate with each other as well as with the teacher, and the teacher learns to communicate with each child as an individual. In this atmosphere, learning becomes an exciting experience for all. In order to create such a learning environment, the teacher needs to have many strings to her educational bow. This is particularly true when she deals with the language arts. One educational string or technique frequently neglected in her training is the use of drama. Although the words "dramatize it" frequently appear in teachers' manuals and lists of suggestions, many teachers do not know where to begin the dramatic process. There is a process by which even those without special training can create an exciting drama learning situation.

This dramatic process may be divided into five steps: sense awareness, movement, characterization, improvisation, and dramatization. These steps should be used as a guide to help the teacher. It is not always necessary to begin with step one and conclude with step five. However, many teachers inexperienced in drama have found these steps a helpful guide in developing meaningful dramatic experiences for their children.

SENSE AWARENESS

As Piaget, the prominent Swiss psychologist (1954) has so carefully pointed out, sensory experience is necessary to all learning in early childhood. It precedes the acquisition of cognitive skills. Sensory learnings, which are usually taken for granted, can be organized into exciting language experiences.

Listening Activities

The ability of a child to receive and respond to auditory stimuli is basic to all language learning. Classroom activities which aid in the development of this ability are important. Placing these experiences in an active and dramatic context may stimulate both excitement and understanding. Listening to sounds in the environment, identifying them, and projecting them into characters, feelings, and stories aid in the development of a child's imagination. Games which help the children discriminate between animal, human, and mechanical sounds can be a profitable learning experience. Activities which provide emotional as well as intellectual discrimination between environmental sounds enlarge the children's capacity to feel.

Looking

In this visual world, sight is very important. The child's ability to identify and discriminate between printed symbols is vital to both reading and writing. Activities which call for the identification and discrimination of objects, people, and ideas in his environment before he deals with their symbolic representation are extremely important. The use of films, slides, pictures, and field trips to enlarge the child's visual horizons, may lead to his interest in acting out his adventures. Helping the child use his sense of sight to project ideas forward and backward in time cultivates imagination, develops communication, and stimulates oral language. Simple games and activities which help the child to become constantly aware of the sense of sight are vital in language arts.

Touching

Activities which help the children identify objects, people, and situations by the sense of touch alone help develop sensitivity to and understanding of their environment. Stretching the imagination to include touch sensations never personally experienced expands language horizons.

Smelling and Tasting

Imaginative experiences recalling both the sense of taste and smell help the children evoke and use sense memory. This may help their dramatic understanding of people and places and may expand their experience horizon, which in turn broadens their language base.

MOVEMENT

Too frequently teachers of the language arts forget that movement conveys meaning. They are caught up in auditory and visual learning and neglect their relationship to movement. How, why, when, and where they move is important to language learning. Dramatic experiences which involve meaningful movement add greatly to the child's total language understanding.

CHARACTERIZATION

Webster's dictionary defines drama as "a composition in prose or verse presenting in dialogue or pantomime a story involving conflict or contrasts of character." Although this does not totally define drama, it does note the core of the dramatic process—characterization. The essence of drama appears in the development of the ability to mentally, emotionally, and physically enact a variety of characters. The ability to put oneself in the shoes of another is one of the great assets which may be developed through dramatic activities. After the children have become aware of their own personal abilities, they can use them to understand and portray others. How would a certain character listen, see, and touch? How would he move? How old is he? What does he do for a living? How does he feel? It is the child's ability to answer these questions that allows him to project himself into another character and grapple with an imaginary experience. This ability, particularly in older children, can lead to a deeper understanding of literature and develop an expanding base for dramatization.

IMPROVISATION

Improvisation is the development of a dramatic situation without a script. Improvisation develops naturally from experiences in characterization. After children have gained some confidence in the characterization aspect of drama they may enjoy trying on a variety of characters in different situations. First the characters may develop through pantomime, then speech and situation may be added, and an improvisation develops. From this development of simple characters and situations, an interest in playwriting may grow. It is suggested that these plays be allowed to develop at the child's pace, rather than the teacher's. The teacher who suggests that an improvisation should be written down might squelch the whole purpose of drama. If, however, a child says that he would like to write an improvisation down as a play, the teacher might encourage him. She should not, however, insist that the children "put on" or "play out" the child's improvisation. Only if the child playwright insists upon a production should it be undertaken. The value of improvisation is found in its spontaneity and on-the-spot development. When an improvisation is written out, it becomes a play. Improvisation should be encouraged.

DRAMATIZATION

When they speak of dramatization, the great majority of teachers think of "putting on a play." For the purposes of this book, dramatization is not the production of a play. It is rather the informal spontaneous dramatization developed by the participants for their own learning. Although the theme and idea may be played out more than once, it is for the benefit of the participants at that moment.

Dramatizations usually develop from experiences in improvisation. The children plan and develop a story line, a situation, a conflict, or an open-ended sequence and act it out. Following the playing they evaluate their efforts, add and subtract ideas, and replay it again in another form. Each playing is different and is created by different players. In this manner the children experiment with a variety of dramatic forms. They develop their skills as actors and playwrights and sometimes as designers, if properties and costume pieces, lights, and sound equipment are available. This truly creative aspect of drama has great merit, particularly for older children. Through dramatization they develop characters, plot, action, and conflict and find a resolution for their own stories.

Another type of dramatization which has great merit is the dramatization of plots created by others. Selecting and developing characters and situations from history or literature and playing out the plots presented by masters is exciting and refreshing. Unfortunately, many teachers start at this level and become discouraged. It is important for children to play out their reading stories and favorite literature stories, but it will be a much more rewarding situation if the process is not rushed. If the teacher will first help the children develop their own personal potential through sense awareness, movement, and characterization experiences, and then encourage dramatization, it is much more likely to be a happy and profitable experience for all concerned.

Geraldine Siks (1958, p. 191) suggests that there are five steps a teacher should follow in guiding the children in story dramatization:

1. Motivating the children into a strong mood.
2. Presenting the story, poem, or idea from which the children are to create.
3. Guiding children in the planning.
4. Guiding children in the playing.
5. Guiding children in the evaluation of their own work.

Chapter 3

The Dramatic Process
in the Primary Grades (K–3)

LANGUAGE ABILITIES build in a cumulative manner. The base for effective use of language is laid in early childhood and is gradually developed. "How well a student fares in, say tenth or eleventh grade, depends enormously on what he was asked to do in the lower grades," writes James Moffet (1968, p. 3) ". . . his past education seems to be more critical than age or ability." If a child is asked in early grades to sit at his desk and accept stereotyped reading and writing and listen only to the teacher, he will develop the ability to sit and accept, not question or participate. If, on the other hand, he is asked to develop his own abilities and learn about his own environment, the people, places, and things that surround him, he will not only learn the basic language skills but an enjoyment in using them. He will learn that talking is more interesting when accompanied by reading, and reading leads to writing and writing leads to more investigation and all learning can be exciting. He will understand that learning is an active, totally involving process that requires his full attention.

It is in the primary grades that the critical language base is laid. The majority of the primary classroom time is involved with the development of language skills. Research has shown that these skills develop in a sequential manner. The diagrammatic drawing of this process as presented by James A. Smith (1967, p. 55) is helpful.

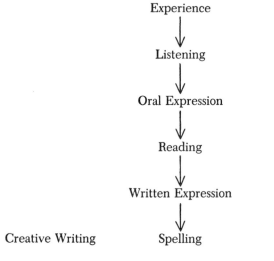

This diagram underlines the meaning of James Moffet's words when he wrote, "Rendering experience into words is the real business of school." (1968, p. 11) The dramatic process can be an invaluable technique as the teacher works to help the child render his own personal experience into his own words.

Primary children bring a tremendous amount of experience with them to school. They have lived for more than five years. Adults sometimes forget this fact and seem to believe that a child's real living begins when he enters the primary classroom. Although many children have what adults assume to be limited language skills, even the shy and neglected child has a wealth of experience. Teachers need to work with him to help him render this past and present experience into words. This means that the teacher must accept noise and much talking along with the children. "To develop their language powers the simple fact is that children must talk a lot. They must use language and use it an enormous amount. Learning to read and write will depend in large measure on the growth of oral speech" (Moffet 1968, p. 45).

A primary classroom can be a wonderful place to talk. Ideally, it is full of exciting things to talk about and play with. There are boxes, blocks and steps of many shapes, sizes and colors and textures. There are many balls—ping-pong balls, basketballs, beach balls, footballs, soccer balls, and rubber bouncing balls. There are nets made of different colors and textures, from elastic to firm cord. There are bats (light baseball bats for indoor play and heavier ones for outside play). There are ping-pong paddles and paddles with rubber balls attached. There are easels with paints and crayons and a variety of sizes of white and colored newsprint and paper. There is a "feel box" full of small articles of different shapes, sizes, colors, and textures. There is a "costume box" full of bits and pieces of clothing, hats, feathers, jewelry, ribbons, and flowers, and a full-length mirror. There is a sink for water play, clay for molding, and a sandbox with many small toys for building. There is Lego, a record player with records, a tape recorder with blank tape, and all sorts of big and little toys to climb on, to investigate, and to use. There are many dolls and puppets, a play house, and books.

This type of primary classroom is an excellent language learning environment. Children, encouraged to investigate this new place upon their arrival at school, take a step in a positive learning direction. Soon the classroom is filled with much talking and reacting. Even the very shy children, if left alone, gradually begin to participate. Small groups begin to emerge and the circular communication system swings into action. The children communicate their ideas and the teacher plays the observer's role as the children become acquainted with each other. She watches as the groups emerge. A group may play in the play house, another group may be at the sand table, while another builds with blocks. Some children may play alone and some may at first just watch.

In the beginning, the teacher interested in organizing such a language learning environment and using the dramatic process will carefully observe each group and enter it only if she is invited. She will try to be as unobtrusive as possible, being on hand to lend support by asking a question, supplying a prop or showing where some item happens to be kept. From this vantage point she can identify the children as individuals and note which children are leaders, which are followers, and which children need courage to enter a group at all. Her observation of the children should be subtle, quiet, and yet supportive. Here she can watch spontaneous dramatic play develop. It is this play and the ideas and material it reveals that the teacher must respect and appreciate if she is to use the dramatic process effectively in the language arts program.

Dramatic play does not need to be taught. It develops very naturally. The sixteen-month old child picks up his daddy's hat, walks to the door and announces that he will "go car." The little girl will put on her mother's shoes and pick up her purse, saying "go store." These are examples of the beginnings of dramatic play. Role enactment appears to be a natural way of reacting to living, even in the earliest years. It grows spontaneously in a rich home and community environment. A school setting full of interesting sights, sounds, tastes, smells, and objects to manipulate forms the fertile soil in which dramatic play can grow. In this setting the child tries on new characters and experiences to see how it feels. A series of wooden boxes may become an automobile and a cap from the costume box may turn him into a taxi driver. Away he goes to pick up his customers to take them wherever they wish. A picture of a tiger on the cover of a book may transform a play area into a wild jungle, chairs become trees, tables become mountains, and away a group of children go on a tiger hunt. A telephone may trigger a scene in a doctor's office, while a cup and saucer might provide a stimulus for a visit to a restaurant or grandmother's home. Playing house, toy shop, football game, or whatever experience is paramount at the moment, is a child's way of investigating his world. He does not always need tangible objects and sounds to stimulate dramatic play. An idea, a word, or a television program can frequently provide the stimulus for much profitable play. Dramatic play does not need to be taught, but it does need to be allowed to grow. In a primary classroom where dramatic play is encouraged language can most easily grow and develop.

SENSE AWARENESS

The first step in the dramatic process, sense awareness, is based on the spontaneous dramatic play of small children. The purpose of this step is to help bring one's senses to conscious level. Active pleasurable sense games can be dispersed throughout the school day providing a change of pace for the children as well as a learning experience. Selecting one sense at a time and spending several sessions on specific sensory games involving each sense may provide much excellent language learning. A good organization for these activities is listening, looking, touching, tasting, and smelling.

Listening

Listening is usually identified as a separate unit of instruction in the language arts. It is frequently listed as one of the neglected skills. However, as a specific part of the dramatic process, that is not the case. Rather than being neglected, it can be seen as the starting point. Two important key principles that need to be kept in mind when organizing listening experiences are: (1) listening activities need to be motivated, not demanded, and (2) listening should not be limited to listening by the children to the teacher. If these principles are kept in mind, the types of listening skills developed in the dramatic process, such as selective listening, critical listening, attentive listening, retentive listening, and so on become less important. It is using the basic skill of listening itself that is important. It is the development of that part of the self that is of prime importance.

General listening needs to be encouraged as a part of everyday classroom living. Listening to stories and poems read by the teacher or recorded by an artist are excellent listening experiences for children and lay a base for more selective specific listening activities. The following listening games are designed to increase the child's capacity to listen selectively and relate meaning to what he hears.

Isolation of Gross Sounds. A necessary listening skill which is basic to all language arts practices is the ability to isolate and identify speech sounds. Beginning with games to identify gross environmental sounds can lay a base for the identification of the more subtle speech sounds. The following is an example of one way a teacher might help her children isolate general sounds and relate them to their stimulus.

"Listen," she might suggest. "Close your eyes and listen. Listen for sounds that are outside this building. When you hear a sound, tell us what is making the sound and keep on listening."

"I hear a car going by the school."

"I hear a dog barking. I think there is going to be a dog fight."

"I hear a jet. It sounds like a 707."

"I hear a truck. It is nearly empty and it is bouncing along."

"I hear a little girl crying."

"I hear the mother calling the girl to come home."

Children enjoy simple games of this nature and they are frequently surprised at how much they can tell about what is happening by merely listening with their eyes closed.

"Now listen for sounds you can hear inside this room," the teacher continues. "Keep your eyes closed and listen. What makes the sound and what is happening?" The teacher now makes a few sounds. She might write a word on the board, open a book, drop a pencil, move her chair, walk quickly across the room and open and close a door, and so on. As she does these things the children can identify the objects used (chalk, book, pencil, and chair) and elaborate by explaining what happened to the object in order to make the sound.

"I hear you writing on the chalkboard with chalk. It squeaks."

"I hear you opening and closing a big book."

"A pencil dropped on the floor. It's a drawing pencil."

"I hear a chair moving across the floor."

"I hear you walk across the floor, open the door and slam it hard. You sounded cross."

"Now," the teacher continues, "listen for sounds inside your-self." This creates immediate silence and gradually the children begin to make such identification.

"I hear my heart beating."

"I hear my throat swallowing."

"I hear my breathing."

"My stomach growled."

Many variations on these gross listening games can be devised, getting more complicated as the children's skills increase. They can provide a change of pace, take only a few minutes and lead to an interest in the development of listening skills. Particularly effective listening games can be organized around mood music and sound effects records. Having the children "explore a cave" as they listen to *2001: A Space Odyssey* may help the children become aware of the auditory space around them. Having children listen and react to selected sounds from sound effects records may help the children pinpoint meaningful sounds within their gross auditory environment.

Relating Meaning to Gross Sounds.   Even the very young children become quite proficient in this type of listening in a very short time. The next step is to give them some games to help them not only identify sounds but to give them meaning. A teacher might record a series of three sounds—for example, a dog barking, the sound of footsteps, and a door bell ringing. The children close their eyes and hear the sounds. "Do these sounds give you a mes-sage?" Almost right away a child will say, "somebody came to the door," "the dog wants in the house," or "the door is locked." There will be a variety of responses, all equally right, if that was the message the child received. Gradually the children make up their own series of sounds and identify the message. The teacher and children together can make up their own sound games of "who is there," "what is it," and "what happened?" Older primary children may also make up a series of sounds to go with the messages, such as "let me in," "where to now," "who did it," and "don't blame me."

Sound effects records are a valuable source of ideas for listening games. A series of environmental sounds listed as "traffic," "bells, whistles, and gongs," "airport," "seashore," and "farm" would help the children not only to identify sounds and their meaning, but also the quality of the sound. It is interesting and helpful for children to identify contrasting quality sounds, such as cross sounds and happy sounds, scary sounds and peaceful sounds. Gradually they become very much aware that they live in a world of exciting sounds.

Listening to television with eyes closed is another simple game which may prove interesting to children, particularly if the program has little speaking. The sound track records of some movies may provide excellent listening experience for the older primary child. A concerted effort to make children actively aware of listening pays dividends in developing all language skills. "What is happening?" the teacher may quietly ask as the children listen to the sound track from *Gone with the Wind.* "What are the people doing?" "Where are they going?" The variety of responses will only add to the overall interest.

Sound stories at this stage are also helpful.[1] Primary children love a story. A sound story is even better because they can actively participate. They make the sounds. "Listen," the teacher may begin. "Watch the storyteller and her magic wand will tell you when to make the sound. It is up to you to choose the sound but it must help the story."

Very simple made-up incidents form the beginning stories. After the children gain some experience, well-known stories can be used. Later, selections from readers, poetry, and their own stories can form the stimulus. An example of an early sound story is as follows. The blanks indicate a pause and the use of the wand to help the children understand when to start, stop, and increase or decrease volume.

---

[1] A series of sound stories and piano sound effects for creative dramatics is available through *New Plays for Children,* Box 2181, Grand Central Station, New York, N.Y., 10017.

Once there was a big forest full of all sorts of animal and bird sounds
————. In the morning at wake up time the sounds began very
softly————and they grew————and grew————until all the birds
and animals were all awake and talking. One day just before wake
up time a big wind began to blow————and the rain began to fall
————and a little lost boy crept into the forest to find shelter. His
teeth chattered————and to warm his hands he clapped them together————and to warm his feet he stamped them on the ground
————. The birds and animals woke up. They heard the wind————
—and the rain————and the boy's teeth chattering————and his
hands clapping————and his feet stamping————. They looked
down and saw the little boy. They talked together————. "We must
protect him," they said, and they did.

From such simple beginnings many more complicated stories
are developed. They can provide a stimulus for even the very shy
child to be a storyteller and direct the sound action with a magic
wand. Teachers and children working together can devise all sorts
of sound games and stories thus stimulating all language learning.

For older primary children the following listening game may
prove particularly effective. It is an excellent small group activity,
which can challenge the imagination of the children and incorporate all the language arts.

First, the teacher records several series of sounds on tape:

Series One: A door slam, a fire siren, a thunder clap.
Series Two: An airplane coming in to land, breaking glass, a
              hum of machinery.
Series Three: Slow footsteps, a dog's bark, general laughter.
Series Four: Waves dashing on the shore, a clanking of chains,
              birds singing.
Series Five: A train whistle in the distance, cry of birds, the
              brakes on a car coming to a quick stop.

Second, the class is divided into small groups. Each group selects
a series of sounds and makes up a story from the sounds. They must
give the story a title and prepare to play it.

Third, each group tells its story before the class. If possible they
may play it out.

Fourth, the children use this sound story to write a poem or a story related to the series of sounds. The story will probably appear in his art work and social studies as well as his language.

Isolation, Identification and Discrimination of Speech Sounds. The isolation, identification, and discrimination of speech sounds is very important at the primary level. The small child needs to be able to isolate one speech sound from another, identify it in words, and be able to discriminate between the different sounds. Most phonics programs are based on this concept. Listening games which can give the children such listening experience are extremely valuable. One carefully organized recorded speech improvement program which is based on this concept is *Listening With Mr. Bunny Big Ears.* It encourages listening through sound identification and discrimination activities, speaking through dramatic play, and reading through emphasis on phonics. The use of this and other programs may be very helpful. However, an imaginative teacher can develop her own speech games.

Children are very interested in their own names. They enjoy identifying the first sound in their name as their sound. Sam's sound is *s*, Bill's is *b*, and John's is *j*. A planned sequence of sound identification games can stimulate much good listening for speech sounds and therefore improve the children's speech. A poem or a simple story which calls for the child to respond when he hears his sound can be interesting. Listening for a friend's sound or the teacher's sound may also prove helpful.

Many primary children have difficulty in discriminating between similar consonant sounds. The difference between *s* and *z* or *r* and *l* may not easily be recognized. This can lead to both speech and reading problems. Therefore, if a teacher organizes some simple active sound discrimination games, much profitable speech improvement may result.

The following story can be listened to in a variety of ways. First, the children can respond (hand clap, hand wave, mark on a paper) every time they hear the *s* sound. The second time they can respond when they hear the *z* sound. The next time the class can be divided into the "snakes" who respond when they hear *s* and the "bees" when they hear *z*. Finally, this very simple story can be played out with half the children playing "snakes" and the other half playing "bees."

As the teacher reads this simple story she must remember that it is the *s* or *z* sounds, not the letters, that the children are listening for. The *s* sounds in the story are underlined once and the *z* sounds are underlined twice.

Once upon a time there was a beautiful forest full of all sorts of snakes and bees. The snakes loved to slide through the long slippery grass. The bees loved to zip around in the branches of the tall trees. "Z-z-z," buzzed the bees, and "s-s-s," hissed the snakes. One day a big boy came into the forest. He was looking for snakes. He wanted to catch one and put him in a cage. Now, the bees and the snakes were friends. As soon as the bees saw what the boy was up to they zipped across close to where the boy stood. Soon the boy saw a snake. "See," he called to another boy, "see, here is a snake. I'm going to get it." But before he could reach down into the grass he felt a sharp sting on his hand. "Ouch," he cried. "Oh, my hand and my nose, my ear. I'm being stung." Out of the forest he rushed and he didn't stop running until he got home. "You are a true friend," said the snake to the bees.

Similar stories or poems can be devised to discriminate between *s* and *sh* or *r* and *l*. These listening games, however, are purely auditory games. The children should not be confused with the visual symbols. They are listening for speech sounds not the printed symbol.

Looking

The world of television, colorful advertising, picture books, and slide shows is a very visual one. Children are constantly bombarded with visual stimuli. Merely looking, however, is not observing, and developing powers of observation is necessary if children are to understand visual symbols. Learning to carefully observe people, places, and things with exactness is vital for the child who is learning to read and write. Activities which place a reward on specific observation skills are exceedingly helpful.

The following looking or observation games have proved to be useful. They are fun for young children and provide an opportunity for them to talk and share ideas in small groups.

What Is Added? In this game the class is divided into small groups of five or six children. Each group chooses ten or twelve objects (a ball, a glove, an earring, a bottle, a sponge, and so on) from the class "feel box." These are placed in the center of the circle, and the children examine them for a few minutes. When the children believe that they can recall and name all the objects, they turn their backs while the teacher or outside player adds one or two similar objects. The game is now to identify the objects that were added. This game can be replayed and repeated with many variations, but the purpose is always the same. It is to help the children observe accurately and discuss their observations. Encouraging the children to add descriptive and comparative adjectives also adds greatly. The glove might become the "grubby brown glove with stains on it" and the bottle might become "the blue bottle which is much bigger than the one in the window." Such advanced identification adds fun and extends the child's developing vocabulary.

What Is Missing? This simple game is a variation on the first one. It may be a little more difficult for small children. They seem to find it easier to identify what has been added than what is missing. This time instead of adding objects, objects are taken away. Extending this game to include pictures, dolls, puppets, and people in a variety of ways adds to the learning value of the activity.

What Is Different? This can be played with small groups or with partners. The object is to closely observe a person or a group, allow for a change to be made, and then try to identify that change. The child or group that correctly identifies the difference wins a point. Puppets and pictures are particularly valuable in this difference game. The "costume box" and "feel box" which should be an important piece of equipment in every primary classroom are extremely valuable in difference games.

How Many? This game is a variation on the familiar "I Spy." It is played in small groups and each child gets his chance to challenge the others. First, the children are given a few moments to look all around the room and select a color, shape, or material. When it is his turn he will ask, "How many blue objects in the room?" "How many square objects can you find?" "How many wooden objects can you name?" The children are given a time limit to see how many they can find in the selected time. This is noisy and rough, particularly if the children need to touch each of their selections. It is, however, fun and can help develop observation.

Follow the Leader. This simple game that every child knows can also provide a good observation experience. Children choose partners and move about the room in slow motion. The follower must observe the leader accurately in order to follow his actions correctly. At the signal from the teacher, the partners change roles. The follower becomes the leader and the game continues. Children must watch very carefully in this game.

The teacher will recognize in these observation games many frequently suggested activities from social science, mathematics, and reading readiness books. This is desirable. The teacher should be constantly aware of the language learning possibilities inherent in all school experiences. Adding dramatic variations to accepted observation experiences can add fun to language learning. Older primary children will profit from expansion of the suggested simple games. The following ideas involve role enactment opportunities as well as observation.

The Observer's Game. The children select from nature, a slide, or a picture the phenomenon they wish to observe. For example, following a brief period for careful observation of the sky the class is divided into four separate groups of specific characters. Their observations are now to be made as those characters. For example, group one may be artists at a painting session; group two, sailors preparing to set out to sea; group three, members of a family preparing for a picnic; and group four, skydivers on a holiday. Each group sees the sky differently. Group one may note the beauty of the clouds against the clear blue sky. Group two might note that there are more clouds gathering in the west. Group three may decide that it is a fine day for a picnic, since the clouds will shield them from the hot sun, and group four may note that the clouds will only add to their diving fun. As the groups discuss the sky in their particular situation, the teacher may take the role of a roving reporter and visit each group to encourage participation from all. If, on the other hand, the children select a man-made phenomenon, such as a highway, the teacher might divide the children into the following groups: group one may be school children at an overpass, group two may be people stranded by a flat tire, group three may be truckers who have been driving since dawn, and group four, foreign visitors in a Cadillac. Again, each group would look at the highway in a different way. Their observations and discussion would vary greatly. Group one might decide to count all the red and blue cars that pass by, group two might decide to flag down a patrol car and get help, group three might decide that the traffic is so heavy that they must leave the highway, and group four might be frightened by the noise and the speed.

The observer's game can be varied by using pictures, slides, film and video tape, as well as nature. Stimulated by observing people, places, and things, they are able to recreate characters and situations. Ideas for observation games are limited only by the imagination of the teacher.

Observing People. This game is usually very popular with older primary children. It utilizes the teacher's picture and slide collection very effectively and challenges the observation powers of the children.

First, divide the class into small groups of four or five children each. Then, present each group with a series of pictures showing people involved in a problem situation. The pictures need to be interesting and able to trigger open-ended questions with a variety of answers. "Who are these people?" "How do they earn their living?" "What are they thinking about?" "Why are they all here at the same time?" All conclusions about the people should be based on some observed detail in the picture. Finally, the group selects the one picture they want to use for the game. They decide *who* the people are, *where* they are, and *why* they are doing *what* they are doing. Each child chooses to be one of the pictured characters in the picture. Then, as the chosen character they decide on a solution to the problem presented and play it out.

One picture which is frequently chosen from an experienced teacher's file depicts a group of tourists stranded in a bus on the desert with a flat tire and a five feet four inch, one hundred and ten pound bus driver. The variety of people, the expressions on their faces, the parcels they carry, the clothes they wear, and the comedy of the situation challenge the children. Interesting solutions to the problem are invented and played out. Inventing biographies or autobiographies for the bus characters is also an exciting writing assignment. Reading and writing as well as speaking and acting out result from this observation game.

Touching

Touch is a very personal sense. It is like taste and smell—very subjective. To one person something may be hard and to another rather soft. Touch depends upon comparison and contrast. A piece of wood might be considered soft when compared with a piece of steel. A dog's bristly fur is soft when compared to a porcupine quill. Because of this quality, games on the sense of touch have tremendous possibilities for language development. Comparison and contrast games to stimulate sense awareness also aid in vocabulary building.

Touch Walk.   First, the children close their eyes and examine everything around them by the sense of touch. They carefully examine the whole classroom and identify common objects by touch. Second, the children each choose a partner. One child is to be the leader and the other the examiner. The latter is blindfolded. With the help of one who can use his eyes, the other slowly examines his environment. The leader must protect his partner at all times and lead him toward things he believes are most interesting. As the examiner identified objects by touch, he reports his findings, and the leader keeps an account of the correct identifications. After a few moments the blindfold is removed, and the partners discuss how he recognized the examined objects. Partners then change roles and the game continues.

The teacher's role in this game can be an active one. She can provide help by side coaching. As she watches the children examine an object, she can help by asking questions. "How big is it?" "What is the texture?" "Is it hard, soft, metallic?" "Is it heavy or light?" "Is it angular or circular?" "Is it porous, solid?" No verbal response is required from the child at this time, but as he examines things through the sense of touch, the teacher's voiced suggestions often increase his absorption and concentration. They also help in his meaningful vocabulary development. The word "porous" may have more meaning for him when he hears the word as he examines the object.

What Is It?   Identifying single objects through the sense of touch alone can also be fun. Have the children form small groups of four or five and sit in a circle with their hands placed behind their backs with palms open. The teacher then places an object in the hand of one of the children. As soon as the child can identify what it is, he passes it on to the next person but he does not say what the object is. When everyone has had a chance to examine the objects the teacher retrieves them and asks each group to describe the objects before final identification.

Variations on this game are many and the children can gain valuable experience as they identify objects by comparing and contrasting shapes, sizes, textures, and weights. Their descriptive vocabulary both spoken and written may increase as they expand their activities and begin to use the dictionary to aid in the game. A series of imagined problems for a blind detective may help the children appreciate and use their kinesthetic sense more fully. Dramatic touch games suggested and developed by the children themselves need to be encouraged.

Smelling and Tasting

By the time the children have participated in sense awareness games using the ears, the eyes, and the hands, they have developed a consciousness of sense impressions. Games and activities involving taste and smell frequently develop quite naturally from previously discussed games and experiences. Helping the child to become verbally conscious of these senses through memory recall may be helpful.

"Recall your favorite smell. Tell us about it."

"You are a sailor out at sea. Suddenly you smell a frightening smell. What is it? Why is it frightening?"

"You are lost in a strange city. What smell would you most want to smell? Why?"

"You have a very bad cold. What would you most like to taste?"

"You are starving. What tastes would you recall?"

The sense awareness games suggested here can be expanded into many language arts activities. Adults sometimes forget that they learn about themselves and their world through developing their senses. Children need to explore and use their sense equipment in order to understand their personal resources. The teacher who wishes to provide exciting learning experiences for her children needs to give them many opportunities to consciously use their senses. As Brian Way (1967, p. 25) writes ". . . our sensitivity as people, our awareness of ourselves and the world about us, and therefore our own personal enrichments in life are all partly dependent on developing our sensory instruments to the fullest extent of their powers, different as these powers might be for each individual."

MOVEMENT

The second step in the dramatic process is movement. People express themselves naturally through movement. Every movement they make expresses something about them. This fact has frequently been ignored when considering the language arts. Linking senses to movement helps the children develop their unique powers of self-expression.

Children frequently say that language arts teaches them to talk "with expression." When questioned, they rarely know exactly what they mean by expression. They do know that it has something to do with how they speak. Rarely do they understand that it has something to do with how they move. If children are to develop their powers of self-expression, they need to concern themselves with expressive movement as well as expressive speech.

In some primary school programs in the United States movement is the key to all physical education. The work of Anne and Paul Barlin *(Dance A Story Series)* in the schools in Claremont, California, is an outstanding example. Much of the movement work in England, based on the work of Rudolf Laban (1968) is incorporated into the drama program as an integral part of the dramatic process. Teachers interested in deeper understanding of movement can profit from viewing films *(Learning Through Movement* and *Movement in Time and Space)* and reading the basic movement books (Russell, 1965; and Boorman, 1969). The classroom teacher who understands that movement is essentially involved in the language arts may add more interest to her work by incorporating movement experience in her language activities.

"Look at your hands," she might suggest. "Can your hands say something?" At this point children usually wave good-bye. Now the teacher can ask what other comments the hands are able to make. She, as the leader, might put her hand up in a "stop" position, or use her hand to say "come here" or "follow me." Soon the children begin to think up many ways their hands can talk. They can work with a partner and discover how much they can reveal with movement of hands and arms. This may lead to the idea of expressing oneself with foot movement. "Stop," "no," and "maybe" are usually the first expressions children convey by foot movements. At this point the children may choose partners and participate in "foot conversations." Such is an interesting beginning experience in expressive movement.

Movement to express feeling is an integral part of the language arts. The teacher might begin this understanding by asking the following questions. "Can your hands say 'I'm happy,' 'I'm sad,' 'I'm lonely,' or 'I'm tired?'" Very rapidly the children begin to realize that emotions can be expressed through movement of hands and arms. "Let me see happy arms and hands, sad arms and hands, frightened, excited, stealthy and mean arms and hands," the teacher continues. "Now let us move around the room in slow motion. As I call out an emotion, let your whole body express it through movement alone. Fear, joy, anger."

These simple beginnings frequently stir an interest in vocabulary building through movement. A few moments here and there throughout the school day linking word concepts, senses, and feelings to movement is a very profitable language experience.

Once the children's interest is stirred, extended understanding of movement and meaning can be very profitably incorporated in the primary language arts program. The Piaget (1954) theory that the young child learns through sensory-motor perception is pertinent at this step in the dramatic process. The children, having explored their sensory abilities, can now link this learning with their developing motor abilities. Dramatic activities in language arts offer continuing language learning through sensory-motor expression.

Brian Way (1967, p. 65) a leader in drama education in England, points out that movement has an important function in the dramatic process. He suggests that "one of the functions of movement within drama is to help every child and young person achieve complete mastery of his or her physical self, thus enabling an emotional harmony to develop regarding their own bodies, on a basis of full personal confidence and sensitivity." Whether it is possible through drama to achieve such heights is questionable. However, most teachers note that the more inhibited, nonparticipating children are frequently those children who use restrictive movement. Maybe movement experience can help such children achieve some mastery of their physical selves. It should at least offer them a chance to relax and relate meaning to movement.

If a classroom teacher understands a few basic movement principles, she may be more able to plan movement activities related to language. Joan Russell (1965, p. 19) analyzes movement under four headings: (1) The Body (2) Effort, (3) Space and Shape, and (4) Relationship. An understanding of these four concepts will help the teacher use movement most effectively in language arts. Utilizing Russell's structure the following are suggestions for body movement activities.

Locomotion is the first body movement activity. There are many ways in which locomotion is observed—stepping, running, rolling, and crawling. Games which encourage the manner of locomotion related to meaning and movement are particularly helpful in enlarging the child's vocabulary.

Elevation is the second body activity. It includes hopping, skipping, leaping, jumping, and all its numerous variations. Turns, such as spinning, pivoting, spiraling, and whirling add to the variety of ways in which body movement can be encouraged and related to language. Rising and sinking activities help the children relate their body movements to space as do activities involving opening and closing, advancing and retreating. Simple movement stories such as the following can be an enjoyable experience and relate specifically to language. As the teacher tells the story, the children respond through movement. (The dashes indicate the long pauses necessary.)

"Once there was a child who wanted to discover what he could do. He wanted to move his body in every way possible. First he took three big steps———but he was used to stepping. He tried running slowly———and then quickly———. But that too he had done many times. "I can roll," he thought, and with that he got down and rolled over and over. "What if I had to go in a tunnel?" he thought. "I'd crawl."———"The surface is slippery. I'll slide."———"I'm coming to rocks. I'll have to jump."———"I see a stream. I'll have to leap."———"Here comes a big wind through that tunnel. I'll whirl."————"I'll spin."————"I'll make a spiral————movement right out into the broad daylight." Down————he fell to the ground. He was tired so he rested for a whole minute. "I wonder how far I can reach," he thought. With that he stood up and stretched————as far as he could. Keeping his feet still, he tried to reach up to the moon————, then he tried to catch the bush that grew at his right————, then the one on the left————. He stretched————and stretched————and finally he collapsed. As he lay on the ground he curled up in as little space as possible. Then slowly opened his arms————, then his legs————. Then back he went into a very small space again. "I'm going home now," he said as he got back on his feet. "I'm going home hopping————, pivoting————, jumping————, and sliding————. I can move my body in more ways than I thought," the boy told his brother.

Simple stories with more plot can be devised by the teacher and children and played by the group as a whole or in small groups. This can give the teacher an opportunity to carefully observe the children and learn which of her pupils have acquired basic movement skills. She can then devise simple games and stories for the benefit of these individual children without calling class attention to their needs.

Helping small children relate movement to basic learning concepts is an aid to the development of language as well as sensory motor integration. Robert E. Valett (1967) lists among others the following movement abilities that are an important factor in basic learning:

1. The ability to maintain gross and fine motor balance and to move rhythmically,
2. The ability to move one's body in an integrated way around and through objects in the spatial environment,
3. The ability to follow directions and to imitate body positions in space.

The classroom teacher should incorporate such simple movement stories as suggested above and design others to integrate movement into the basic language learning of small children. Soon the children will wish to make up their own stories for their classmates to play and enjoy.

The second heading in the Russell analysis of movement is effort. Here she is concerned with the attitude of the child to the motion factors of weight, time, space, and flow. Story adventures that enable the children to experience weight as strong, light, delicate, heavy, airborne, and buoyant, help to build the child's word vocabulary as well as a vocabulary of movement. Time can also be experienced in adventure stories when time concepts—sudden, leisurely, slow, quick, prolonged, and unhurried, are explored. Space pathways can be explored in action as children follow each other through direct, straight, wavy, flexible, plastic, broken, or threadlike paths. An understanding of rhythmic flow can be investigated as found, controlled, readily stopped or free, fluent, or abandoned. Together the teacher and the children might develop the following simple story using these concepts and play it out in movement.

Once a group of boys and girls were playing on the school playground. They decided to have an adventure. First they tried on their equipment to be sure it was in good working order. They tried on their space suits ———. They walked around in their heavy metal boots ———. All of a sudden they became buoyant ———. They went up and up ———. Now, instead of heavy steps, they made delicate ——— space walking movements. They made a long leisurely ——— prolonged ——— exploration. Then all of a sudden they fell straight down ——— and landed back on earth again. "My space suit is in good order," one boy said. "Now, let's try our underwater equipment." Off came their space suits and on went their diving equipment. Soon the children were down under the water. Leisurely ——— they made wavy paths ——— flexibly weaving ——— through the water. Slowly they pushed aside the seaweed ——— and investigated the rocks ———. Suddenly a big shark swam by. The children in an abandoned manner ——— left what they were doing and darted ——— up to the surface. "That was a narrow escape," the children cried. "Let's stay on earth."

So they walked slowly ——— then quickly ——— then leisurely ———. They made a broken path over rocks ———, then stopped suddenly ——— to miss a snake, then continued to walk over a pile of slippery stones in a controlled ——— manner. Finally the bell rang and the children ran a direct ——— route into the school.

The third heading in the Russell analysis is space and shape. Stories which take the children through experience where they explore space and shape and extend themselves through different levels and in different directions can be exceedingly helpful in relating movement to meaning and language. The children can listen attentively to the teacher's voice as her directions (full of action words and ideas) call for a physical response. Five minutes or so spent in such active language activity may pay dividends in the development of basic learning abilities. The concept of space in movement, left and right, up and down, forward and backward, is also important in reading, writing, and arithmetic. Being able to differentiate in size and shape are vital in the three r's. Using the whole body to express these differences is often very helpful. "Can you make your body into the shape of a 'T', an 'S', or a 'Y'? Let me see two children get together and make the letters 'W' and 'M'. Make your initials with your body. Divide into groups of four and let your bodies make these shapes: square, triangle, rectangle, and circle." Simple short activities of this nature may help build the small child's concept of himself in space. Once a teacher begins such simple games, many more ideas will come to her. As one six-year-old explained his five-year-old brother's liking for movement games, "He likes it because he uses his whole self." Giving the children the opportunity to use their whole selves aids not only in developing language but the whole child.

The fourth and last heading in the analysis is relationship—the relationship of the body parts, the relationship of individuals, and the relationship of groups. Here in the development of movement relationships, opportunity for language is high. Games that involve telling relationship stories in movement can be very effective.

The teacher and children can develop such stories, play them, and evaluate them. The following ideas in sentence form may challenge older primary children and help them develop relationship concepts in movement.

"I am lost. Help me."

"I'd like to get to know you."

"There is going to be a storm."

"It is only a haunted house."

"Where do we go from here?"

Working together the children learn how to express ideas in movement. In order to do this they must work together and develop relationships that can be expressed without words.

The use of movement experiences in language arts activities may add more life and meaning to listening, speaking, reading, and writing. Active energetic children need to move. If their physical energy can be thus incorporated, profitable language learning for all may be attained.

CHARACTERIZATION

The first step in the dramatic process, sense awareness, aims to develop the individual's sensory understanding. The second step, movement, aims to develop physical movement skills and to integrate them into the necessary sensory-motor abilities so important to all learning. The third step, characterization, aims to utilize the previously emphasized sensory physical abilities and help develop the drama skill of role enactment. In order to do this, special emphasis is placed on personal speaking skills and their projection into many characterizations.

Conscious awareness of people is the beginning of characterization. Observing people carefully and asking ourselves how they feel, move, speak, and react to the what, where, and when in their lives is the first step in characterization. Viewing television news shows, watching crowds at a bus stop or a ball game, and separating individuals from the group for special consideration can spark an interest in characterization.

The teacher who has a large picture file of people and animals readily available in her classroom is best prepared to introduce the concept of characterization to children. First, she should divide the children into small groups of four or five. A large selection of "people" pictures is given to each group for examination. The children are to look at the pictures very carefully and choose the two they consider most interesting. Active discussion among the children should be encouraged as they select their pictures. Going quietly from group to group, the teacher might ask pertinent questions to stimulate their talking. "Do you see anyone you know?" "What is happening?" When each group has chosen its two pictures, the class reassembles to discuss the selections. The teacher encourages their talking by inserting questions into the discussion at short intervals. "Who are these people?" "Where do they live?" "What are they doing?" "Why are they doing this?" "What are they talking about?" "What is going to happen?" "Which person do you think is the leader in this picture?" "Why do you think this?" "What do the others think?"

When the children have had an opportunity to freely discuss the people in the pictures and are beginning to zero in on one or two interesting characters, the teacher may gain their attention and assign the next step.

"Look carefully and choose the person you would like to be," she begins. "I choose to be this lady and I am going to have a party in my big house. I invite you all to come to my party as the person you choose. Before you come to my door be sure you have decided exactly *who* you are, *what* you are doing here, and *why* you have come. Take a few moments to choose who you will be." After a brief pause, the teacher can open the imaginary door to her house and welcome the visitors. An informal scene will develop, noise will be great, but if the teacher is observant, she will be able to find the children who need encouragement. As the hostess (not the teacher), she enters the playing and carefully draws these children into the scene. As the hostess, she can control the events, assigning appropriate duties to her guests according to their characters. The shy little boy who chose to play the bus driver might be given a plate of imaginary cookies to pass around, and the very verbal little girl who chose to be the haughty lady might be asked to give special attention to a child who chose to play a frightened, timid old man. The party continues until the hostess brings the party to a conclusion and the guests leave.

These beginning group experiences can be noisy and unfocused, but they help the children stretch their imaginations and begin to think about role enactment. They help the children understand what is meant by "staying in character."

Group scenes such as the one just described can deteriorate into chaos and result in very little learning. It is in the discussion period which follows the playing that the real language arts learning takes place. This evaluation needs to be positive and concentrate on the good things that happened. The teacher might open the discussion by saying, "That was a very interesting party! I'm glad I decided to be the kind lady and have a party. Did you enjoy it? Who did you meet at the party? Oh, do you think an old man would do that? Why?" As the discussion proceeds (and it should be brief), the teacher emphasizes the basics of characterization—the *who* are you?—*where* are you?—*what* are you doing?—*why* are you doing it? Following this evaluation, the replay of the party is likely to be more focused, and the children will begin to become the characters. Spaced throughout the school day, simple characterization games can be a help in developing drama activities. The following suggestions can be adapted in many ways and become vital language activities.

Who Are You?   Simple group games can be developed from a dramatic stimulus presented through pictures, slides, television, books, community events, or the children's own ideas. Before playing a character game, the children must know "who" they are going to be. For example, they may decide to be giants. They must be given a chance to try on this character. The children need to move freely about the classroom. The teacher may side-coach by quietly asking, "How big is he? How does he move? What would he say to his neighbor giant? The giants are in the woods. A storm is coming. What will they do?" Each playing may be followed by a brief discussion on the characters and what they would do if they played the character again. Suggestions to add music or a drum beat should be followed, particularly if a child suggests it. The teacher should accept all the children's suggestions for "making it better." She can turn out the classroom lights (if they are ghosts or some other shadowy creature), use simple sound effects and in every way stimulate concentration and imagination. Even a few bits and pieces from a costume box, a hat or a book may aid the "who" games. As long as the properties do not take over the activity and become more important than the participants, they should be accepted. The active participation of the children as they become absorbed in their playing and sincerely try on characters is the focus at this point.

Where Are You?   Following some emphasis on the who you are, the where should be added. Have the children suggest characters such as a fireman and then let them explore where they are. Expect the children to decide on the environment and imaginatively explore where they are. Side-coaching is often helpful. "How big is the hose? Is it round? Is it heavy? What is on the floor? Are the walls rough? How is the air?" Such questions asked quietly and initiated by what the children do can frequently establish a "where" very successfully. The experience gained in sense awareness games is brought into play in this step. Keeping in character the children frequently discuss problems that arise from the where. "My hose is stuck," one fireman might say to another. "Help me get it out." "I will as soon as I finish washing the fire dog. Here, stand still." "Maybe we should wash this truck. The fire bell might ring any moment." Encourage the firemen to stay in character and concentrate on where they are. Many excellent playing out experiences such as this frequently develop into an increased interest in reading specific stories, or travel books, or writing news articles about places, people, and things. Emphasis on "where" when established by a well discovered "who" can be an exciting learning adventure.

What Are You Doing?   This step can be rather hectic. Stimulated by pictures, objects, or children's ideas, participation can be exciting. For example, a group of cowboys (who) can be in a corral (where) branding cows (what). Or a group of tourists (who) can be on the beach (where) watching some dark clouds (what). Much discussion and planning may precede the playing. The children know that there are many different types of cowboys or tourists. They have to decide who they are before they go into the where and play what.

"I'm going to be a rich tourist who is old and grouchy," says one child.

"What made you grouchy?" asks the teacher.

"I lost some money," the child may reply.

As soon as the children have decided on their characters they will need to consider what kind of a where it is. If they are tourists on a beach, they may discuss what type of beach and what is on the beach (such as sand, rocks, cliffs, a boat house, and so on). With the who and the where firmly established and knowing that they are watching a black cloud, the playing can begin. Conversations among tourists result as we see the different characters examining the environment for shelter. Some tourists may play a game of dodge ball, another tourist might take a nap, and still another, a swim. Activity and talking should be everywhere. Frequently the opportunity for the teacher to introduce an unplanned "what" appears. Then as a character she can enter the playing, provide the stimulus and observe the reaction of the players. For example, she could come down to the beach as the mayor of the town and announce that all tourists were to be sent to jail for questioning. Hopefully, the children would respond in character (who), pick up their belongings, and protest the injustice. At first the unplanned event and character may break the children's concentration. However, after a few experiences they begin to find satisfaction in being able to continue playing without a break. Sometimes a child who is not in the current action may enter the playing and add to the happening.

Why Are You? This is an evaluation step. As the children become more proficient in being characters, reacting to an imagined or real environment, responding to a situation, they become somewhat analytical about their work. The "why" of the character becomes interesting. In the beginning a child might say he was a "sad, old man." With experience he is more likely to explain that he is a "sad, old man whose children have left him." As they think about characterization they think more about cause and effect. Third-grade children who have had considerable characterization experience frequently become quite perceptive about the characters they play. This type of expansion of ideas and rounding out of characters has a very real effect upon the children's oral and written expression. Through thinking about the characters and analyzing their thoughts, feelings and actions, many observable language benefits may be derived particularly with older primary children.

IMPROVISATION

Improvisation is the development of a dramatic situation without benefit of a written script. For the purposes of this work it is usually a situation which develops out of the imagination and at the instigation of the players. With primary children improvisation is really a more polished type of dramatic play. It develops naturally from activities dealing with characterization.

Following activities involving animal characterizations, a group of primary-age children might decide to improvise a scene in a farm yard, a circus tent, or a pet shop. No set plot would necessarily appear. The children would first play out their ideas, possibly discuss it, and even decide on some type of plot structure. Here the responsibility of the teacher is to guide but not direct. A carefully placed question by the teacher is more helpful than a definite suggestion. The following account of an improvisational experience of a group of second graders may serve to define improvisation and the teacher's role in its development.

The second-grade children in a suburban school were very interested in the circus. A television program initiated their excitement and pictures and films shown at an assembly brought their interest to a high peak. The teacher selected many story books about the circus and placed them in a prominent place in the library corner. One child brought a clown costume to school and another some white clown make-up. Instruments in the rhythm band took on a new excitement, particularly the cymbals. Jugglers, sword swallowers, band leaders, bare back riders, strong men, clowns, and dwarfs appeared.

"Let's have a circus right here," said the class leader.

"How could we do that?" asked the teacher.

In the free discussion period that followed, the children decided to think of a circus character and see if the teacher could tell who they were.

"Fine," said the teacher. "Do you think I could help you in any way?"

"How about playing that record?"

"You mean the circus band music?"

"Yes."

"Alright. Anything else?"

"Yes, you be the voice on the loudspeaker so we'll know when to start."

"Fine."

"Ladies and gentlemen," announced the teacher-narrator. "As soon as the band begins to play you will see before your very eyes the world's best circus characters."

As the music flowed from the tape recorder, the children became the circus characters. There was no set form to the activity. Every child listened to the music and responded to its rhythm. The teacher watched as the sword swallower held the flaming sword aloft and plunged it in and out of his mouth; the leader of the band high-stepped all around the classroom and bowed frequently to the imagined crowd; the juggler kept a series of eight imaginary balls in the air; the trapeze artist did cartwheels and somersaults and a variety of other circus characters were all intent on doing their best.

When the music stopped the children looked eagerly at the teacher and asked, "Could you tell who I was? What did you see?"

The teacher explained what she saw, identifying the characters she had observed. "I saw sword swallowers. My throat felt hot just looking at them. And I saw band members—a trombone player, a drummer, and guitarist. The players all followed the beat very well. I think I saw a snake charmer and several very funny clowns. One was really clumsy."

"Did you enjoy the circus?" the teacher asked the children.

"Yes," the children agreed.

"It was too confusing," said one child.

"What could we do about that?" asked the teacher.

Many ideas were suggested. Finally one child said, "We need to all walk in the same direction. I saw a circus, but they walked in a circle and didn't bump into each other the way we did."

"Oh," said the teacher. "You mean we need to decide where we come in and where the circle leads us and where we go out."

"Yes," said the children. "We need to come in at that door, go around the room and out that door again," one child decided.

"We need some people to sit in the grandstand to watch the circus parade and cheer," one little girl suggested. "I want to be the mayor and all the circus people must bow to me as they pass."

"That's a good idea. I'll be the mayor's wife," said another child.

"And I'll be his bodyguard," announced another.

The children decided to be a variety of characters not previously incorporated in the circus.

"Just a minute," said the teacher. "You'll need to help me here. If I am the announcer, I'll need to know who is going to be who. How will I know that?"

"I don't know—maybe we could have name tags," suggested one child.

"No, not that," said another.

"You be the doorman, Miss Brown, and stand at the door. As each person enters, he can tell you his name."

"Good idea!"

"Oh, I see," replied the teacher. I'll be the barker and call out the names of the performers. I can still run the tape recorder too."

"And we will come in and bow to the mayor and go around the circus ring and back out the other door," explained the vocal leader.

"I see," the teacher admitted. "The barker will know when to start the music as soon as you are all ready."

The result of this group improvisation was delightful. The children built several other improvisational scenes around the circus theme. The children's art, as well as oral and written language, reflected their interest. The whole classroom was alive with the circus for several weeks.

The circus interest waned somewhat when a child brought some arrowheads to school. Circus improvisations faded and were replaced by Indian folk lore. Soon the circus books were forgotten, and books on pioneers and Indians took their place. The children became immersed in native Indian culture. Pictures, films, and records inspired new improvisation ideas. At first these were somewhat unfocused, but gradually an organization of their ideas appeared. Stimulated and guided by the teacher's careful questions, the second-grade class at Cloverpoint improvised many pioneer and Indian themes.

Improvisations also stem from children's ideas. "A summer day," "a visit to the museum," "an Indian camp fire," might trigger some delightful experiences in improvisation. Ideas arise at different times throughout the school day and when possible should be acted upon. In the beginning the teacher needs to remember that there is a "scribble stage" which must be lived through. Initial improvisations rarely have any set form—a beginning, middle, or end. All the children talk at once, and it is difficult for an observer to get an idea of what is going on. However, the important fact for the teacher to remember according to Brian Way (1967, p. 186) "is that because the improvisation has been made up by and then done by the group, they do know what is happening. They are not communicators, actors, or playwrights, so that in the early stages they will lack clarity in communication." Gradually some form will begin to appear, the children will listen to each other, make concrete suggestions about "what happened" (conflict), discuss a "high point" (climax), recall the feeling (mood and atmosphere), and evaluate the players (characterization). These elements of dramatic plot evolve if the teacher is patient. If she realizes that her purpose in using creative drama in the language arts is not to develop actors, productions or playwrights, but sensitive, communicating children, she will allow the improvisation step in the dramatic process to proceed at the children's pace. In some cases improvisation may lead rather quickly into dramatization; in other cases, it may not.

DRAMATIZATION

Dramatization for the purposes of this work develops out of the children's interest in improvisation. Whereas in improvisation they develop dramatic experiences out of their own ideas, in dramatization they use the work and ideas of others. That is not to say that the children do not use their own ideas in dramatization.

They always expand and develop their own ideas. But, in the dramatization step the original idea (story or poem) to be dramatized is usually the work of someone else. For example, the before-mentioned improvisations developed on the circus theme might lead to the dramatization of a circus story, such as, "The Little Clown Who Lost His Laugh" (Ward, 1952, p. 73). This very simple story has a plot with a conflict, a climax, and some very interesting characters. It is ideal for dramatization by young children. Many characters can be added to the original story and different scenes can be developed, but the basic form is the work of the author of the story. Stories and poems from readers can be used for dramatization. The basic difference between improvisations and dramatizations is to be found in the initial stimulus. When the stimulus comes from a poem or story written by someone other than the participants it is considered dramatization.

An improvisation can be developed from a wide variety of ideas. This is also true for dramatization. However, some poems, stories, and historical incidents lend themselves to dramatization and others do not. Certain specific qualities need to be present in a story if dramatization is to be most effective. The type of story does not appear to be nearly as important as the qualities inherent in the story and the children's immediate interest in it (McIntyre 1969, p. 153). This is particularly true with the primary-age children. When they are interested in a theme or a story, they are very, very interested.

Dramatization of a story is frequently considered to be the main aspect of creative dramatics. Without any previous preparation on the part of the teacher or the children, a teacher jumps in to dramatize a story. Very unsuccessful experiences have resulted from this practice. The following case in point may serve to illustrate the problem and encourage the inexperienced teacher to proceed more slowly and give the children the suggested preparation.

A young teacher in an urban school wanted to "do dramatics" with her first-grade children. She had heard that the children "just made up their own words." Since they all knew the story of "The Three Bears," she decided she'd begin with this story.

"Today," she told her children, "we are going to make a play out of "The Three Bears." You all know the story. Tommy, you be Papa Bear; Joanne, you be Mama Bear; and Kelly, will you be Baby Bear? Elizabeth will be Goldilocks. Come up here in front of the class. Here are the three chairs. You play out the story."

The four children came to the front of the room and looked at each other. The teacher was surprised when one said, "I don't know what to say." The teacher had observed some very fine dramatic play in the play corner. She had chosen the children she had seen actively participate. Now in this suggested situation placed before the rest of the class they didn't know how to react.

"Go ahead, play the story," she encouraged.

"We don't know how," the children said.

"That's the last time I'm going to try creative dramatics," the teacher reported to me. "The children just stood there. From here on I'm going to forget this creative bit and write out a play for them to memorize. Creative dramatics just doesn't work."

Fortunately, after some observation of more experienced teachers at work and reading about some of the needed techniques, she decided that she would try again.

"I see now I jumped into the middle of the process," she reported later. "I put the children on the spot. They didn't know where they were, who they were, or what they were supposed to do. Now I know that a great deal of work in sense awareness, movement, and characterization needs to precede improvisation and dramatization."

The class this teacher taught the following year profited from her previous experience. The children played sensory games, shared ideas through movement, and improvised characters from pictures, films, and objects. Finally, after several months when she asked them if they'd like to dramatize "The Three Bears," the result was completely different.

The children all "tried on" the characters of the bears, they moved the way the bears would move, discussed what bears might talk about and they set up the bears' home in the middle of the classroom. They knew the environment because they had planned it. They knew the characters because they'd been thinking and talking about them. They dramatized the story because they were well prepared for the experience. The whole class profited because it was an interesting development in their learning process.

The teacher reported that she had learned more than the children. She learned to start at the very beginning of the dramatic process and proceed at the children's pace. She learned also that there was a skill to the selection of material suitable for dramatization. Not every story or poem lends itself to this form of presentation. Some stories need to be read and enjoyed for the beauty of their words alone. They do not always lend themselves to dramatization. Only when dramatization of a story can add to its interest for the children should dramatization be encouraged. Winifred Ward (1952, pp. 4–6), a founder of the creative dramatics movement in the United States suggests that a good story for dramatization should include the following qualities.

1. The *idea* should be of some worth, and the writing carefully done.
2. The central situation should involve *conflict* of some sort.
3. There should be essential *action* in the development of the plot and it should be action which can be carried out satisfactorily.
4. The *characters* should seem real, whether they are human or animals with human characteristics.
5. The situations should call for interesting *dialogue*.

Generally, the best stories for dramatization in primary grades have vital characters, considerable dialogue, a lot of action, and follow a simple plot. When the children suggest that they wish to make a play from a story, it usually contains these characteristics. Encouraged by previous playing of drama games, their first dramatization attempts are frequently successful and very satisfying.

You, as the teacher, might want to refer to Geraldine Siks' five steps in dramatizing a story (See page 12). The inexperienced teacher may find these steps particularly valuable. When the teacher's manual states "dramatize it," the following elaboration may be of assistance.

"King Midas and the Golden Touch" is a well-loved children's story which fits the selection criteria for stories to dramatize. There are in this story many characters of interest to primary children. Besides the little princess, the strong, powerful and selfish King Midas, and the supernatural stranger, Mercury, there is an opportunity to create additional characters, such as friends for the princess and servants for the king. There is much action inherent in the story and it has an exciting climax. The sequence of events in the plot leads logically to a successful conclusion. Therefore, "King Midas and the Golden Touch" is used here to show the five-step cycle in dramatizing a story.

The first step, "motivating the children into a strong mood," is partially accomplished in the process of selecting the story. The children will have already given some indication of their interest in the story material, or it would not have been chosen. This particular myth is well-known to most children, and it is one of their frequently requested favorites. The motivation step in this case is not difficult.

There are many ways to set the mood and thus motivate the children. The most frequently utilized is through a general discussion. The following questions might stimulate some ideas. (1) What do you value most? (2) If you had only one wish, what would it be? (3) What is a myth? (4) Do we make up myths today? (5) In your opinion, what is the best characteristic a human can have? and (6) What is the worst characteristic?

Presentation of slides to set the mood is frequently effective. There are some interesting films and film strips[2] of ancient Greece and its gods available. A discussion of ancient gods and their purposes also stimulates child interest. A talk by a community visitor who has spent some time in Greece might set the mood for the telling of the story of King Midas. Once the children are interested in ancient Greece and its gods and myths, they listen carefully to the next step.

---

[2]Encyclopaedia Britannica Educational Corporation, 425 North Michigan Avenue, Chicago, Illinois, 60611, or Britannica House, 151 Bloor Street West, Toronto 5, Ontario.

Telling a story you wish children to dramatize is usually preferable to reading it. All primary teachers should be good storytellers. They should plan very carefully and practice telling the story on tape before telling it to the children. The story must be told so that the characters come to life. The action and setting must be clearly defined, and the plot line easily followed. The telling should be as long as is needed to make it exciting but brief enough to catch the enthusiasm of the moment. A story being told for dramatization must stimulate action. The children should be motivated to want to play out the story. If pictures or objects help make the story exciting, they should be used. The story, however, if it is a good one, should be able to stand alone. Looking directly at the children and using as much dialogue as possible the storyteller must make the characters come to life. The aim in telling a story for dramatization should be to have the children see the story happening as it is told.

Following the telling of the story plans for the playing need to be made. The children should be eager to begin and want immediate action. Instead of discussion it is sometimes wise to begin by having the children "try on" their favorite character.

"Which character did you like best?" the teacher may begin. "Don't tell me, think about it and choose the character you thought was the most interesting. Now, when you are ready, I'll give you a signal, and you become that character. Do what you think he or she would do on a bright sunny morning. Ready? Begin."

If the teacher observes carefully she might see a gleeful king counting his money; a princess picking flowers in the garden; the god, Mercury, leaping through the air, or a servant bowing before the king. On the other hand, she might observe a king walking slowly in his garden examining the flowers with dissatisfaction; a princess playing hopscotch with a servant's daughter; the god, Mercury, perched on the high peak, Mt. Olympus, watching the world below. There may be considerable talk and noise and an opportunity for the teacher to enter this playing as a servant, a caller, a duke, or whoever seems appropriate in order to involve all the children.

"King Midas' court, let us all come to the garden," the teacher might call out when she wants to bring the players back to the classroom. When the children are quiet, a brief discussion of who they were is in order. She might add to the discussion by suggesting, "I saw one very greedy Midas. He looked very stern as he counted his gold. I saw a princess who really loved that garden. I could tell by the way she picked and smelled the flowers."

"I don't think the princess would pick the flowers," one child might suggest. "She'd order a servant to pick them. That's what I did."

"That would make the princess mean like her father," another child might add.

"We all see the character in different ways," the teacher might interject.

"Did you like the way I was Midas, Miss Jones?" one eager young man might ask.

"I saw several King Midas'. Each was a little different. But what I liked most was that they all seemed to be real. I didn't see Bobby, John, or Terry—I saw King Midas."

"What kind of a King Midas would you be?" a child might inquire.

"If I was Midas, some of you servants would get a raise in pay. You were so polite."

"What about the others?"

"I think I would fire a few of them. Those rough ones—they'd ruin the king's dishes," the teacher might quietly reprimand the show-offs without mentioning names. "Let's discuss the characters. Let's talk about the king first."

"I was a kind king, but a greedy one. That's why I smiled but kept the door closed when I counted my chest of gold."

"I was a sad king. I'm not happy because I don't have enough gold."

"Any other ideas about the king?"

"He is very proud and walks very straight and speaks in a big gruff voice."

"That's an idea. Any other suggestions?"

"I think he's absent minded, because he thinks about gold all the time."

"Alright. Let's sum up these ideas about King Midas. He is stern and maybe absent minded. He is proud and talks in a gruff voice. But, above all, he is greedy. Now, what about his daughter?"

"I was a very happy princess who liked to play all day with other children. That's why I grabbed Judy's hand to have her dance with me."

"I was a kind of sad princess because my father didn't let children play with me."

"I was a very proud princess who ordered everyone around."

"Sounds to me as if Marigold could be played in many ways according to what the players wanted," the teacher may sum up. "What about the god, Mercury?"

"I was a god like a ballet dancer," one child might offer.

"I was a god who was cross and just sat up there and watched over the earth," another might suggest. "That's why I climbed up on the ladder. I was on the top of Mt. Olympus."

"I think Mercury would be light and fast sometimes, and sometimes he'd just sit," a thoughtful boy might add.

"Let's have six servants in our playing. Two for the king and four for the princess," the class leader, eager to get the action started, might suggest.

"Good, these are some fine ideas!" the teacher might encourage. "You have many thoughts about *who* will be in the story. Let's talk about *where* this story will take place."

"It should be in the king's garden."

"No, it should be in his counting house."

"I think he might have a special counting house set up in the garden."

"That's a good idea. The garden is all around, and the counting is over there."

"That big key in the 'feel box' is the only key that can open the counting house door."

"What I want to know is where is the big palace," the teacher might inquire.

"It's back there, out of sight. All you can see is the gate to the garden," explains one of the children.

"Very well," said the teacher. "Sounds like good planning to me. *What* is happening when the playing begins?"

"The king will be watching the princess play in the garden. Then he'll go in to count his money."

"That's when Mercury will appear and grant him his wish."

"Fine," says the teacher. "Now we know *who* is in the story, *where* the story takes place, and *what* is going to happen to start the story."

Let's choose who is going to play who the first time," suggests an eager child.

"Let me see," says the teacher. "Do we have six volunteers who would like to be the servants first? Good, now you servants set up the garden and the counting house while we choose the king, the princess, and Mercury."

After the characters are chosen and the garden and counting house in order, the playing begins. There are likely to be several children not in the playing for the first time. They have, however, a very important part: they are to observe with two specific ideas in mind. First, they are to note what is particularly good in the playing, and second, they are to watch for ways it could be made better when they play it again. They know that there are many different ways to play a story and that observers learn too. They also know that they'll get their turn to play a role later.

As the story progresses, the teacher may enter the playing, but always as a character. Sometimes the story goes off at a tangent, and this character (the teacher) may get it back in focus. For example, during a first playing of King Midas, one of the servants may take over and begin a whole sequence of gardening problems. This is .excellent and should be encouraged up to a point. When the teacher believes that the idea of transplanting the whole garden has gone on far enough, she might enter the playing as the head gardener and suggest that the servant go into town or that the king needs help with the lock on the door of the counting house. As a character, she shifts the focus so that the planned story can proceed. She never calls out directions from the sidelines as the teacher. Always her actions are in character as long as the playing proceeds. Her serious attitude and active participation toward the activity helps the children concentrate on their roles and on their responsibility for bringing the story to a successful conclusion.

The completion of the story should be a high point in the dramatization. If the children have really been involved, there will be an exciting ending. King Midas' realization that Marigold has come back to life should be a happy moment.

"Marigold," he might cry, "you are alive."

"Yes, Papa, of course I am."

"What a relief," the king might sigh. "I don't care if I ever see gold again."

Following the playing out of the story, a discussion is held. Although the children sometimes want to say what is wrong with the playing, it is a good idea to begin on a positive note.

"What characters did you see, John?"

"How did you know he was the king?"

"Where were the characters?"

"How did you know they were in the garden?"

"If you had not heard the story before, would you know it now?"

Keeping the questions open-ended and directed toward *who, what, where, when,* and *why* usually brings forth some excellent comments and suggestions for the next playing.

"I knew John was King Midas by the way he walked. He held his head high and looked sideways at the servants."

"I liked the way the princess laughed and skipped."

"I saw Mercury come in on a cloud. When he whirled round and round, I could feel the wind. His voice was spooky like the wind, too."

After the children have had an opportunity to talk about the positive ideas, the teacher might ask, "Are there any suggestions to help make our next playing even more exciting?"

"Yes, we could have some music or a gong when Mercury comes in."

"How about more conversation between Marigold and her father?"

"What would they talk about?" asks the teacher.

"Maybe she hasn't finished her school work."

"Maybe she wants a new dress."

"Maybe she wants to go and play next door," the children may suggest.

This evaluation-discussion step is of particular importance. Here concrete suggestions for the replaying are evaluated and decided upon. The opportunity for the children to express their own ideas and then put them into practice immediately is excellent. It is very easy for the children to get side-tracked in such a discussion. The teacher should try to keep the evaluation meaningful and concentrate her questions on who (the characters), what (the plot), where (the environment), and why (the complications). The type of evaluation that suggests competition should be avoided. The competition, if any, should be with oneself.

"I think I was a better King Midas than I was a servant," one child might say. "I like to give orders."

"Not me," another may reply. "I liked being the servant. I can think of more ideas for a servant than a king. I'd rather play a servant."

A dramatization such as I have described may be extended over several language arts periods. As long as the dramatization is of interest and the children's characterizations are developing the same story is appropriate. Over the years I have seen very exciting adventure stories develop from very simple beginning plots. I watched the nursery rhyme, "The King of Hearts," develop into a child's detective story and become an exciting part of every school day for nearly a month. The final dramatization of the rhyme was in three separate scenes.

The first scene was in the queen's kitchen as she and her servants and cooks prepared for a great baking contest: who could make the best cherry tarts? The scene ended as the queen realized that the tarts she was to enter in the contest were stolen.

"Call the palace guards," she cried.

The second scene was in the palace garden where the search for the tarts and the thief was proceeding. The scene ended as a soldier overturned a big box and discovered the missing tarts hidden behind it.

The third scene was in the king's throne room where the king, aided by judges, was trying to unmask the villain. The knave was discovered when a servant noticed that he had cherry jam on his hands. He was brought before the king who beat him. The knave then promised not to steal again.

Every child in the class contributed to the development of this story dramatization, and the activity created a great deal of other language interest. Stories were written about the tarts, the kingdom of hearts, and the value of corporal punishment. The school librarian reported an increase in the reading of stories about kings and queens. The teacher noted some unusual art work. Several children attempted to write their own rhymes. It was their interest in trying to "play out" some of these invented rhymes that led to the final playing of the knave of hearts.

Dramatization of a story can be a very important part of creative dramatics. It is not, however, the only aspect of drama. If it is to be truly meaningful and help the children develop their artistic and language skills, it needs to be the result of much prior work. If activities involving sense awareness, movement, characterization and improvisation precede dramatization, the experience can be much more rewarding. Dramatization can then be a "living through" experience. Without that background, dramatization frequently becomes a teacher-directed, teacher-coached, talking out of a story. Dramatization at its best is the living through of a story guided, not directed, by a teacher.

Chapter 4

The Dramatic Process
in the Intermediate Grades (4–6)

IT IS ASSUMED that the teachers of the intermediate grades have read the preceding chapter which dealt with the dramatic process. The process is the same throughout all grades. The facility with which the older children deal with the process will depend to a great extent upon their previous experience. Many of the suggested activities in the forthcoming section are continuations and expansions of the primary work. Teachers in the intermediate grades whose classes have not participated in drama should adapt sense awareness, movement, characterization, improvisation, and dramatization activities as suggested for the primary children before proceeding to more advanced work.

By the time the child has reached fourth grade he has usually mastered the basic language skills of listening, speaking, reading, and writing. Less concentrated class time is spent on the development of the language arts as separate subject areas. However, by now the child begins to realize that all learning depends to a great extent on language. Instead of separate listening, speaking, reading, and writing classes, his language experiences are focused on a broader base. The teacher's language arts emphasis should now be on the development of communication skills, interpretative skills, and problem-solving skills. It is at this stage that the use of dramatic techniques may be most valuable. They may serve as an integrating force between language and other learnings.

Dorothy Heathcote of the Institute of Education at the University of Newcastle in England defines a teacher as "one who creates learning situations for others." This section will attempt to show how a teacher can create learning situations using the dramatic process and thus help children develop their communication, interpretation, and problem-solving skills. The examples described are not presented as strict models to follow. They are furnished as a stimulus to the imagination of the reader. Every teacher will approach the actual experiences with her own particular bias and interest. She will react with her own group of children and together they will develop their own dramatic experiences. The following examples, however, may help the teacher focus her activities on the language and drama goal she envisions.

DEVELOPMENT OF COMMUNICATION SKILLS

Communication is defined in the American College Dictionary as "the imparting or interchange of thoughts, opinions, or information by speech, writing, or signs." The development of communication is inherent in the dramatic process as the child explores his ideas and feelings through sense awareness games; translates these understandings, information, and opinions into characterization, improvisation, and dramatization activities, and develops an understanding of nonverbal language (signs) through movement experiences.

Communication skills according to Frank B. May (1967, p. vii) are necessary for self actualization and constructive citizenship. He claims that one of our biggest educational mistakes is the focusing of classroom learning upon the communication *acts* of listening, speaking, reading, and writing, instead of the serious problems of communication. Communication as dealt with in this publication is considered to be a circular flow of nonverbal and verbal information, ideas, images, and attitudes between a source (the child or adult willing to share) and the receiver (the child or adult willing to attend) (Galvin and Book 1972). To help the teacher provide children with learning situations where the language focus is on communication rather than on language acts is the purpose of this section.

The Dramatic Process and Communication in the Fourth Grade

The experience of an imaginative young teacher in a semirural area in the midwest is presented here as an example of the use of the dramatic process and the development of communication skills at the fourth-grade level. The children in this particular class had participated in many dramatic activities in the primary grades. They had played many sense awareness games, improvised stories to music and creatively developed a story for presentation to their parents. Because of their past experience the children frequently requested drama. At the same time another request was heard. This was for a sample paragraph of each child's creative writing. It was to be a noncorrected example of the child's spontaneous expression. One of the criteria by which these contributions were to be judged was "the communication of ideas, feeling, mood and opinion to the reader." The children were supposed to be unaware of the competition involved. A young, enthusiastic principal who was an English major in college had committed the school to a county-wide investigation of elementary writing.

The young fourth-grade teacher did not want to pressure her young children. On the other hand, it was her first year of teaching and she wished to please her principal. She decided to capitalize on the children's interest in drama and her need to provide the principal with examples of good creative communicative writing. Using her understanding of the dramatic process (sense awareness, movement, characterization, improvisation, and dramatization) she planned the following experience.

The sense awareness step in the dramatic process emphasized listening. First the teacher divided the class into several small groups of approximately five members each. The groups were then told to find a comfortable space in the room and sit down and relax. As soon as all the groups were quiet and ready to listen, the teacher played a recorded sequence from *The Grand Canyon Suite* (sunrise sequence). The children listened and imagined how the music made them feel.

The movement step involved the simultaneous group expression of the way the music made them feel. The feeling was expressed in movement and no speech. The members of one group appeared to be slowly waking up from a long sleep. Another group appeared to be sneaking across a wide expanse, while another group appeared to be floating in space. Each group member had his or her own interpretation of what the music meant to him.

The characterization step followed naturally from the movement and it included both the listening of the first step and the movement of the second. Again the teacher asked the children to listen to the same selection of music. This time, however, they were to listen and think about *where* (environment) they felt they might be, *who* (characters) they felt they might be, and *what* (crisis) they imagined might happen. Following a common decision on their environment, characters, and crisis, each group was to plan an improvisation in pantomime which would communicate their ideas to the rest of the class.

The presentation of their ideas constituted the improvisation step in the dramatic process. Each group had its turn. As the music played and the class watched, the performing children tried to communicate their ideas to the watching children. Success was achieved when the watchers grasped the performers' ideas of who they were, where they were, and what had happened. The members of one group were Arabs lost in a hot, dry desert, and who found an oasis in time to prevent disaster. Another group were cowboys on the early morning trail. They discovered a lone bald eagle and tried to shoot him, but they were relieved when the bullet failed to hit its mark. A group composed mainly of boys were astronauts lost in space. They finally found a space station. The members of another group were underwater sea divers looking for treasure. At a crucial time a hose sprang a leak. The last group presented a very exciting incident. As pirates they sneaked through marsh and swamp and were struck by cannon fire as they reached the deck.

Following this improvisation step the class broke up into groups again. Now their assignment was to prepare a dramatization which included speech and present a conclusion to their improvised adventure. This dramatization step was completed a few days later. The first group dramatized a scene in an Arab chieftain's tent. Following the discovery of the oasis the travelers learned that they had broken a law by taking the water. They were forced to pay a large sum of money before they could return to the airport to board a plane for home. In order to satisfactorily complete this step, the members of the group had to read rather extensively about deserts, Arabs, and oases. This, no doubt, was further stimulated by the television presentation of Laurence of Arabia.

The second group which had elected to be cowboys was also influenced by the television medium. Their presentation revolved around a courtroom where they were being questioned concerning the use of fire arms, the possible extinction of the bald eagle, and air pollution. A suspended sentence and a fine culminated their early morning experience.

The third group appeared to know a great deal about space. Their scene evolved around a communication problem between earth ground control and the space station. It included a space walk and discussion of interplanetary travel.

The fourth group presented a very exciting scene on the deck of a ship. The divers had brought up news of a great sunken treasure. Following the exchange of a new hose for the leaking old one, the divers again descended, while their wives dreamed of the treasure they were about to obtain. The scene ended with an argument between two of the women being interrupted by the return of the divers with a sample of the "treasure." It turned out to be a bag of bottle tops, instead of pieces of eight.

The fifth group concluded the dramatizations by switching the focus of their previous improvisation. Instead of being the pirates, they were the sailors preparing to set sail. Their plans, however, were disturbed by the arrival of a band of pirates who prevented the sailors from firing the warning shot, and they sailed away with the ship and its crew.

Lively discussion followed each dramatization. The importance of communicating specific ideas and feelings became apparent. Excitement was obvious when communication between the sender and the receiver was clear.

"It was a lot of fun," said one child.

"It's work to get your idea across," said another.

The following day the children were asked to write their "sample" of creative writing. Recalling the excitement of the previous days when the dramatic process had aided in communication, the children began to write.

Before the selections were presented to the principal, the young teacher read some of the children's work. It was liberally sprinkled with the adventures of pirates, deep sea diving, astronauts, and cowboys, but it communicated originality, imagination, and excitement to the reader.

It would be a fine ending to this story if I could say that the fourth graders won all the prizes in the contest. They did not. They did, however, warrant some unusual comments.

"These children have a feeling for words."

"What imaginations!"

"Unusual use of picture language!"

The teacher was rewarded. She believed that she had successfully integrated all the language "acts" of listening, speaking, reading, and writing into successful communication.

The Dramatic Process and Communication in the Fifth Grade

The following example of the dramatic process and its utilization in developing the communication skills of intermediate age children concerns a fifth-grade group. The members of this class, however, had had no primary school drama experience. Their present teacher spent several months working with the children to develop their basic drama skills. Using the activities generally suggested for the younger children, but using more mature ideas and material, she established drama as an important part of their school program. One of the language activities they enjoyed was a game called "Titles." It developed from a picture collection to which all the children had contributed. "Titles" consisted of entitling and retitling these pictures. In the beginning a picture of a red barn at sunset was entitled, "The Red Barn." Gradually that title for this picture was changed to "Evening Hush," and finally it became "Once It Was." The children were continually adding pictures to their gallery and retitling them.

One day the teacher suggested that the children choose eight of their favorite people pictures. She then divided the class into four small groups and gave each group two of the chosen pictures.

"Explore the pictures carefully," she said. "Decide who the people are, where they are, and what they are thinking and doing. As soon as you have decided on the who, where, and what, turn back the clock one half hour before this picture was taken. Decide what would be happening then. Make a tableau of that incident. Be sure you communicate the idea so that the rest of the class can give a title to your tableau."

Group one had chosen a picture of a group of tired people on a bus. One man couldn't find his wallet and was being ejected to the consternation of the rest of the passengers on the bus. The children's flash back tableau was a scene in an office where the man was playing "big shot" to the girls in the office as the office boy relieved him of his wallet. Their title: "Vanity, Vanity."

Group two had chosen a picture of five school boys looking innocent as a mouse jumped out of the teacher's desk drawer. Their tableau showed five school children being scolded by the teacher for being late to class. Their title: "All that Fuss for Just Ten Minutes."

Group three had chosen the picture of Tom Sawyer sitting on a barrel counting his loot as the other boys did his work. Their tableau showed Tom being teased by the boys because he had to work. Their title: "He Who Laughs First Laughs Least."

Group four had chosen a picture of a group of tough western characters counting money. Their tableau showed a stage coach hold-up. Its title: "Share the Wealth."

The children enjoyed the game, discussed the merits of their ideas and suggested that with the second of their two pictures they set the time clock an hour ahead. Others suggested playing out what happened between their tableau and the picture. Others thought of stories they would like to write. One little girl, who had been in the Tom Sawyer group, wrote an eight line poem entitled, "What's Not Work."

Communication skills are developed in such language activities. Children begin to understand the underlying principles of the sender and the receiver of the message. They learn that communication is completed in a variety of ways. The teacher can develop many imaginative approaches for using the dramatic process to stimulate communication—pictures, tape recorders, video tape, radio, and television are usually suggested. They are not, however, as readily available as the newspaper. By the time children have reached the fifth grade, reading the daily newspaper should be a regular part of their life. Use it.

News items in our daily newspapers contain many dramatic situations. They can provide an excellent communicative stimulus for dramatic activities. One fifth-grade teacher integrated her language arts and social studies periods into a very profitable project. The children brought newspaper clippings which they found interesting and which they believed communicated a specific feeling. These were not to be the big national stories, but rather the human interest type of news release. The children searched through the newspapers and found some very interesting material. One girl found a brief story about a child being saved from a fire by the barking of her pet dog. A boy was impressed by the rescue attempt of one boy to save another stranded on an ice flow. Another child was interested in the experience of an unemployed man who found a wallet and turned it in to the police. In this class these human interest items formed the basis for drama.

First, the class was divided into small groups for selection and discussion. The news items referred to above were chosen. The children decided that the actual reported happenings were not to be focused upon. Instead, their improvisations were to be the result of the reported incident.

Second, each group was instructed to prepare an improvised scene which could have happened following the reported incident. They were to show the mood and feeling of the environment as well as the mood and feeling of the characters. The incident was to be brought to a satisfactory conclusion. This did not necessarily mean a happy ending. The children decided, however, that the conclusion must be logical and possible.

Third, the groups were given several days to work out their ideas. They played out several endings and finally chose the one to be presented to the whole class. There was considerable confusion and noise. The children did not appear to be distracted and the members of each group were so busy that they paid relatively little attention to the other groups.

Finally, the improvisations were presented, discussed, and evaluated on the basis of believability of environment, character, and incident. Competition was eliminated. No group was to be ranked above or below another. The whole experience was a learning situation for all.

In the case of the rescue from the fire, the improvisation became the scene in the insurance investigator's office. Here, the real hero, the dog, was identified. This improvisation required a good deal of research on the part of the children, including a visit to the class from an insurance adjustor (the father of one of the children). The second group decided to make an improvisation of the scene where the boy hero received a medal for his bravery. The third improvisation concerning the lost wallet was a scene in the man's home before he turned the wallet into the police. In each case, issues were raised, library research was required, decisions had to be made. The newspaper became a living communication.

A similar idea involving television news items proved rewarding but somewhat less effective. News items from the radio provided excellent stimulus, as did the work of a ham radio operator who visited the class. The need for effective communication became apparent to these children. The value and interest of extending oneself beyond the actual stimulus dawned on this fifth-grade group. They had used the dramatic process as a vehicle to extend their understanding and knowledge and in so doing developed all their communication skills.

The Dramatic Process and Communication in the Sixth Grade

Another example of the expanded language experience that the dramatic process can stimulate can be seen in the following experience of a sixth-grade class. Again, the children in this group had had some primary drama experience. They had played sense awareness games, explored movement and meaning, and investigated characterization, improvisation, and dramatization. They frequently suggested that they use drama to aid their understanding of historical figures. Their classroom was an active, exciting learning environment. Paintings, films, and news events frequently initiated dramatic investigation.

One day a wooden replica of "The Praying Hands" was brought into the classroom. The children examined the wooden sculpture and began a discussion on the importance of the sense of touch and character. The children examined their own hands and the hands of their classmates. They carefully examined the hands in pictures. Some of the children brought in pictures of historical events and examined the characters according to their hands. One boy began to make a list of all the personal qualities hands revealed. He soon had a long list including work worn, heart rending, calloused, angry, fearful, vicious, powerful, weak, excited, careless, and transparent.

As the children examined their hands, they discussed characters and consulted the dictionary on expressive words and thus expanded their useable vocabularies. The teacher went to her "feel box" and arranged a variety of objects on her desk. There were rocks, both jagged and smooth, minerals, feathers, pieces of driftwood, a variety of pieces of cloth, fur, and net. There was a large, antique key, a battered box with a broken lock, a stick with a hooked end, large chunks of colored glass, sponge rubber, and play dough. There were great contrasts in color, texture, weight, size, and shape.

The class was divided into three smaller groups. Each group selected three items from the desk. The assignment was to build an improvisation around these three items. The emphasis was to be on characterization and the sense of touch as they related to the three items. The children worked very hard in their groups, paying no attention to the members of other groups. They talked earnestly, examined the items minutely, developed dialogue, accepted and rejected ideas, and finally decided on their improvisations. The teacher reminded them that their improvisation must communicate who, where, what, and when, but she didn't direct their efforts. Several times she was called into discussion with each one of the groups, but she usually answered their questions with another question. She guided, but did not direct.

The following day the groups presented their improvisations before the whole class. First, they showed the items around which they built their improvisation, indicated any other important information, set up their environment, and proceeded.

One group chose a feather, a metal ornament, and an old cane. The narrator told the observing group that they were to turn their clocks back in time to about 1600 A.D. and to imagine they were in Italy. Then, placing a stepladder in place, he picked up the cane, bent over slightly, rubbed his hands over the cane and shuffled back and forth shaking his head.

"It isn't possible," he said in a cracked voice. "He just wants to stir up trouble. What Aristotle says is so, is so. Dear, dear."

Two "young" members of the group soon joined him, and it was obvious by their scrolls that they were students. They waved their hands, argued, and showed in every way that they were excited. They opened their imaginary scrolls. One eagerly touched the document, but the other was less caring.

"You'll see Galileo will be right," the eager one insisted.

A moment later another member joined the group. He had two items in his hand: a feather and a brass ornament. He was accompanied by several others who watched with awe. They all examined the feather and the brass ornament and talked excitedly, commenting on the size, weight, and shape of the objects. One of the crowd was blind and needed assistance, and the students gladly helped him examine the objects as they discussed the great experiment Galileo was about to perform. Tension and excitement built up as Galileo climbed the tower (ladder), carefully protecting himself and his material from the now angry and hostile group. Then, from the top of the tower, he dropped the objects. A great stillness and expectation came over the crowd. As the objects touched the floor at exactly the same time a gasp was heard.

The old man picked up the items. "It can't be true," he gasped, as he examined them. Two of the students shook Galileo's hand and jumped for joy, but the others glared and slipped away.

A second group had chosen an old box, the big, antique key, and a bright piece of molten blue glass. Their improvisation was in pantomime. Their chosen environment was underwater. They had selected soft slow music to aid their efforts. The whole scene was in slow motion, but the story line was very clear. Four of the children were sharks and three were deep sea divers. The divers were examining the wreckage of a ship in search of treasure. One found a treasure chest and a key to open it hidden under some seaweed. On carefully opening the trunk, he took out a large jewel and placed it in a flap of his wet suit. He then called the other two and showed them the chest. These two examined it and then took it up to the surface to investigate their loot. The thief who planned to keep the jewel for himself stayed below looking for more jewels. Suddenly the stolen jewel cut through his suit, and he began to struggle. His air supply was in danger and, as he thrashed around, the sharks found him, destroyed him, and left the jewel lying there. The children succeeded in communicating all these ideas without saying a word. Their exploration of the undersea environment was exceedingly interesting.

The third group chose a piece of driftwood, a silk cord, and a tattered piece of white cotton. Their scene took place on the rocky shore of a deserted island. The members of this group were the survivors of a shipwreck. Their dialogue showed that they had been washed ashore a week before and had been arguing ever since. They had used their hands to build a shelter, had climbed trees to get food, and had dug a well for water. But then they had begun to lose hope of rescue. From their dialogue it could be learned who they were, what they feared, and why they wanted to be rescued. There was a wealthy plastic surgeon who resented having to use his hands for such rough work. He wanted to be rescued because he was such a valuable person in society, and he didn't want his wife to collect the $100,000 life insurance. There was an artist who had found the driftwood particularly beautiful. He wished for his tools to make artifacts from the wood. "I could make a million," he kept saying. There was a newspaper reporter who kept talking about the great story he could write if rescue would only come. He wanted to keep busy and used his hands to build sand castles. There was a young lady who was greatly annoyed by the reporter. She hoped to become a great movie star, and she didn't want to ruin her hands by working in case they were rescued. "Maybe someday they'll take a close-up of my hands," she claimed. There was an absent-minded old gentleman who had lost his glasses in the wreck. He had to examine everything minutely in order to discover what it was.

In the course of the improvisation a ship was sighted. Everybody had to cooperate in order to get the piece of cotton on the silk cord and waving, so that the captain of the ship could find the stranded crew. The characterizations were clearly drawn and their dialogue and action told their story. The rescue was accomplished and a relieved, but more understanding group departed from their island.

The foregoing examples, stimulated by the first step in the dramatic process (sense awareness), culminated in using other steps (movement, characterization, and improvisation). Speech and movement skills were evidenced throughout as the children communicated their ideas to those who watched. Every child participated and the language arts experiences that followed these initial improvisations were extensive. The children read about other early discoverers in order to identify characters who would make good playing. Some began to investigate the undersea possibilities and hidden treasure. They located sunken treasure maps and tried to find out how a diver would go about rescuing it. They took an interest in reading about survivors, and *Robinson Crusoe* and *Swiss Family Robinson* appeared on the library shelf. The contents of the encyclopedia and other reference books concerning these improvised adventures were researched. Here the teacher had provided learning situations where the integration of language arts focused on communication rather than on the individual language "acts" of listening, speaking, reading, and writing.

These examples are presented not as models for the teacher to follow. They are presented as a stimulus to trigger the teacher's own ideas and imagination. In the next twenty years there will be a technological revolution in the classroom, particularly in communication. Children will still be expressing themselves with pen, paper, and pencil. But to this they will have added the typewriter, the video tape, and the film, and other communicative systems not now in production. Their ability to use tape and film to express their ideas effectively will depend to some extent on their ability to communicate through the dramatic process. The elementary child of today may be producing a film in high school in lieu of a term paper. He may be listening to audio tapes in lieu of reading reference books. He may be taping some of his themes instead of writing them. If this is the case, the understanding and experience he can gain in his early years dealing with dramatic techniques will be of great value. The young, inexperienced teacher should create learning situations for both her children and herself—thus allowing her use of the dramatic process to develop communication skills.

THE DEVELOPMENT OF INTERPRETATIVE SKILLS

In 1955 Paul T. Rakin (pp. 103–106) made an analysis of the frequency of adult language activities. He discovered that the average adult spends 70 percent of his total waking hours in some form of communication. Of this, 11 percent of his time is spent in writing, 15 percent in reading, 32 percent in speaking and 42 percent in listening activities. From this it may be concluded that since listening and speaking constitute the greatest proportion of adult communication it is vital to emphasize the development of listening and speaking skills in elementary language arts programs. The dramatic process, which is dependent on both listening (sense awareness) and speaking (characterization, improvisation and dramatization), encourages the development of these necessary skills. Through careful guidance of dramatic activities a teacher may help children in the intermediate grades develop high standards of speech excellence, evolve and express their own ideas in stories, poems and plays, and appreciate and interpret the literary works of others.

The Dramatic Process and the Development of Expressive Speech

Interest in the factual content expressed in listening and speaking activities begins in early childhood education. By the time the children have reached fourth grade, however, their expanded experience makes them more aware of the feeling and quality of listening and speaking activities. They begin to understand that how they speak is important. They realize that speech tells a great deal about how a person feels and what attitudes he holds as well as what he has to say. The development of speech, which not only conveys the message and the feeling, but is also pleasant to hear, becomes a reasonable language goal.

Charting Speech Change. Since speech is an acquired skill, it is possible to analyze it and work on change and improvement. In order to chart change, however, children need to have a base from which to begin. Therefore, at the beginning of the school year a sample (tape recording) of each child's speech should be recorded, dated, and preserved for later comparison. The recording needs to be brief and recorded under relaxed conditions. Children should choose their own selection and have a chance to practice before it is recorded. If, however, a child would rather talk spontaneously, that too should be acceptable. It is obtaining a sample of the child's speech at the beginning of the term that is important.

Following the recording the teacher should play back each recording individually. She should discuss the recording with the child and have the child tell her what he likes or dislikes about his speech. Together they can decide on some listening and speaking activities from which he may profit. For example, one child might decide that he "mumbles," another that he talks "too fast," another that his voice is "dull," "too low," or "too high." The teacher does not need to confirm or deny the evaluation. She and the child need to plan some individual activities to help remedy the dislikes. The teacher can profitably suggest that all learn from listening to good speech. She should suggest that the children listen to television and radio announcers, recordings of poems and plays, and so on, and listen carefully to the speech of the performers. Each child needs to have his own particular listening project. The child who believes that he mumbles will listen for mumbling. As he listens he will ask himself if the speaker mumbles. The child who thinks he speaks too fast might use a stop watch to time the speaker. The child who says his voice is dull will listen to hear if others are dull. As the children listen with their own purpose in mind, they concentrate on the speech of the speaker. Gradually they become more aware of voice quality and speech in general. As long as this listening is an interesting, personal game, children will benefit. Since each child's project is individual, no comparison with other children is necessary. The whole procedure is to make the children aware.

After three months of listening and many drama activities where speaking is involved, a new series of recordings should be made. The children compare their new samples with their old and see where there is obvious change and improvement. Because of the listening emphasis there is frequently a marked difference. If the child believes he has improved, he has. Because he believes this, the teacher should not suggest otherwise. The purpose of the recordings is to help the child become personally conscious of the quality of speech. If he has become aware, improvement will follow. A different way of listening has opened to him. Hopefully he has a different attitude toward speech. He has become perceptive.

Individual and Group Listening and Speaking Activities. "You cannot overestimate the importance of reading aloud to children at every age," reports Professor Johan Aitken of the Faculty of Education at the University of Toronto. "I've asked many college students which elementary school teachers they remember most fondly and why. Very often they remembered the teacher who read stories to them. It was one time they could hardly wait to get to their classrooms. And it is one of the times a teacher feels most intimate with her class" (Quig, 1973). Listening to stories and poems read aloud by an interested teacher forms a basis for many other exciting activities. Every classroom teacher should learn to be a good oral reader. This takes practice. Practice with a tape recorder and a live audience. The effort put into becoming a good reader pays dividends in personal satisfaction and child enjoyment and learning. There is no substitute for this valuable listening experience and it should be a regular part of the daily routine— a shared listening time where communication between teacher and child is felt.

Excellent individual and group listening experiences are also available in recordings by outstanding performers. Many publishing companies have developed programs and individual presentations which serve as exciting models for listening.[3] Wherever possible a listening corner with play back instruments and ear phones for individual listening should be provided. The models of speech presented have multiple values. Literature comes to life, adventure is available and horizons are opened.

With excellent models which the teacher and the recording artists provide, the child's interest in his own performance increases. Here the tape recorder is very valuable. By encouraging each child to record his reading or talking and listen to the play back, the teacher may persuade even the shyest child to perform. If his first efforts are attempted and evaluated by himself alone, he may gradually gain confidence and share his efforts with others.

The dramatic process is particularly valuable at this point. Small groups of children may develop characterizations around an interesting improvisational scene. For example, a fourth-grade group decided to record the work of a roving reporter. They decided who they were, and the question that was to be asked. Because

---

[3]Some of them are Weston Woods, Weston, Conn., Encyclopaedia Britannica Educational Corporation, Chicago, Ill. Educational Activities Inc., Freeport, N.Y. Educational Reading Service, Paramus, N.J., and The MacMillan Company School Division, N.Y.

they were currently interested in the visit of a diplomat to Washington, they decided that they would be government employees going to work. The roving reporter would interview them at the door of their office building. Using the tape recorder and some sound effects, the scene was recorded. Each child became the character he imagined and answered the reporter's questions as he believed the character would reply. The following dialogue was recorded.

(REPORTER): I am standing on the steps of the office building in Washington. It is a bright day, but it is cold and windy. Here, sir, can I talk to you?

CHILD 2: Yes, yes, what do you want?

(REPORTER): I'd like to ask you what you think of the visit of the Russian?

CHILD 2: Russian? What Russian?

(REPORTER): Why, the diplomat who is coming to town today.

CHILD 2: Never heard of him, I just mind my own business. Goodday.

(REPORTER): You, miss, can I ask you a question?

CHILD 3: I'm almost late for work and besides it's cold out here.

(REPORTER): It will just be a minute. What do you think of the Russian visitor?

CHILD 3: I think he should be given a big party to impress him.

(REPORTER): Why is that?

CHILD 3: So he'd go home and say what nice people we are.

CHILD 4: Here, miss, don't talk to these reporters. It might get you into trouble.

(REPORTER): That's all, folks. I'll have to move on. The crowd has gone in.

Following a play back of this interview the children discussed their work. They analyzed their characters and decided that they really sounded like themselves. They talked about what they might have done to make the characters come to life. Finally, they replayed the scene. Then the reporter interviewed a group who had witnessed an imaginary accident. The children specifically planned what they believed had happened. Their ideas were enhanced by the reading of a newspaper report of a recent local accident. Each participant decided exactly who he was and why he was interested in telling what he knew. The recording that followed was lively and exciting. The children listened to the play back with much more interest. This time they noted the feeling behind their words.

"Your voice tells a lot about you," one child commented, as the session ended.

The following week the children decided to write some short dialogues and record them with different moods behind the same words. The following dialogue was recorded four different times in four different moods. The first time the characters were "exhausted;" the second time, "excited;" the third time, "frightened;" and the fourth time, "angry."

SCENE: Inside a space ship in flight.
CHARACTERS: Two astronauts, Joe and Bill

JOE: Find it?
BILL: No.
JOE: Have you tried the left switch?
BILL: Which one?
JOE: The green one, stupid.
BILL: Don't call me stupid.
JOE: We had better contact ground control.
BILL: Why? Do you think we are lost?
JOE: Could be. Ground control —— Come in —— Star Flight calling ground control ——
BILL: Keep trying.
JOE: I think I hear something.
BILL: Great! What?
JOE: Quiet! Ground control, come in ——
BILL: Keep it up. It's working.
JOE: Yes, I hear you. Push them both at the same time.
BILL: Like this?
JOE: It worked. I get the message loud and clear.
BILL: We made it.

Each recording was carefully discussed and replayed. The children noted that although the same words were said with each playing, the meaning behind the words differed greatly according to the mood. When the exhausted astronaut said, "Have you tried the left switch?" it really didn't matter. However, those same words spoken in an excited voice changed the whole concept of the dialogue.

The fun and excitement enjoyed generated more dialogues, some written and some spontaneously devised and recorded. In this manner active listening and speaking generated a new awareness of speech, mood, character, and what can be revealed through speech alone.

The wide variety of listening and speaking experiences available is limited only by the imagination of the teacher. A series of recorded telephone conversations between well known people both living and dead might prove particularly interesting.

"What would you hear if you listened in to a telephone conversation between Queen Elizabeth I and Queen Elizabeth II? What would Leonardo da Vinci have to say to a local artist? How would the mayor of your town talk to Christopher Columbus?" Taping such conversations would require considerable research on the part of the students. The possibilities for learning are almost unlimited.

The reading of the imagined diary of Davy Crockett, Admiral Byrd, or whatever men or women currently being studied in social science might prove an exciting and worthwhile project. How would a twentieth century reporter conduct an interview with a man from the past such as Julius Caesar? How would a man from the future write about the men of today? Many such dramatic activities challenge the children and call for work in all the language arts!

Choral Speaking and the Dramatic Process. Choral reading is one of the language arts activities frequently suggested for all children. It is considered to be a synchronization of three important elements of language—listening, reading, and speaking. When carefully planned, it may develop the interpretative skills and a broad appreciation of literature.

Marjorie Gullan (1931, p. 2) who is considered to be the person who revised the ancient art of choral reading in the twentieth century, says that it can be taught as "a means to an end or as an end in itself." A teacher may use choral speaking as a means of improving the speech of her children. In this instance she will not consider the choral performance as only an artistic product. She will emphasize the value of the learning experience as she works with her children to prepare the reading. In this manner she uses choral reading as a means to an end. The means is the preparation of the choral reading and the end is, hopefully, the improvement of the children's speech. Another teacher may use choral reading as an end in itself. At all times she will have the product, a well rehearsed group interpretation of poetry or prose, firmly in mind. If some by-products, such as improved speech accrue, that is fine. However, her chief objective, that of creating an artistic product, remains her chief goal.

Whether the teacher uses choral speaking as a means to an end or as an end to itself, the phases through which she guides her children are similar. The following is an excerpt from a speech given by the writer at a language arts conference several years ago (McIntyre 1965, pp. 71–75). It explains briefly and concisely the most important ideas behind the teaching of choral speaking in the elementary grades.

The teacher who is to make the most effective use of choral reading must understand its basic philosophy and phases before she attempts to use this method. There are many pit falls and both teacher and pupils may easily become discouraged. To prevent this, a teacher needs to learn how to work with the tools of choral reading and place the whole experience in a proper perspective. Before she attempts to lead a group of children she must learn for herself the progressive phases through which a choral reading project passes.

The first phase is the understanding of rhythm and tempo. Little children who delight in nursery rhymes are not interested in the words or the meaning. It is the rhythm, the flow of the words and the pattern of the flow that delights them. The first step in their appreciation is the opportunity of feeling the rhythm. There are many ways in which this may be explored. The children may clap, sway, skip or beat out the rhythm. Skipping out the rhythm of Jack and Jill, clapping out the rhythm of Hickery Dickery Dock and swaying to the rhythm of Little Boy Blue offers the children a chance to feel and become part of the rhythm. Encouraging the children to suggest different ways to express the rhythm of nursery rhymes is a broadening of their experience. Frequently the shy child who might be afraid to speak out by himself may happily join in the adventure of discovering the rhythms which underlie simple rhymes. Gradually the teacher may point out that the rhythms may be fast or slow, happy or sad and slowly the concept of tempo becomes a part of the rhythmic pattern. The purpose of this phase is to encourage the child to sense the rhythm and tempo through the whole body. Older children may not find the nursery rhymes the proper vehicle for discovering rhythm and tempo. There are simple rhythmic poems which are admirably suited for this purpose. The lilting rhythms in the words of A. A. Milne, Rachel Field or Eleanor Farjeon are valuable. Exploring the rhythm and tempo underlying A. A. Milne's "The King's Breakfast" may prove to be lots of fun. At this stage the teacher is not too concerned about the interpretation of the material. She is interested in having the children feel the rhythm and tempo which underlies the work.

The second phase which the teacher must understand is the color and quality of voices. She needs to understand the meaning of the choral reading terms. It is not necessary that the children know them as definitions but the teacher needs to be aware of them. She must know that (1) *inflection* is the rise and fall within a phrase and (2) *pitch levels* refer to the change between one phrase and another (3) *emphasis* is the pointing up of the most important word and (4) *intensity* is the term used to indicate loudness and softness of the voices. These terms will have meaning for her as she reads about the art of choral reading. Many texts may suggest lists of exercises to help make voices more flexible. But others may indicate that isolated exercises have little if any "carry over" into the art of choral reading. Where there is no underlying meaning there appears to be no experiencing. Therefore, instead of isolated exercises to help develop the color and voice quality it is suggested that the teacher use exciting, simple material. When the development and understanding of inflection and pitch levels are related to the meaning of words within a poem instead of a mechanical exercise, something happens. Children learning to be sensitive to pitch, inflection and intensity are more likely to comprehend and enjoy the experience if they are learning through a poem such as "I Have Known Rivers."

The third phase that the teacher must understand is the arrangement. This is the orchestration of the choral reading. It is the creative aspect of the project. Here the children and the teacher work together to find the best arrangement for emphasizing and clarifying what the poet meant to convey in the poem. The teacher needs to understand the different ways in which this meaning may be expressed. The poems that have been pre-planned and orchestrated by some authority may have some value. The readings that have been arranged by the children and teacher working together have much more value. Before the teacher can lead a group of children in the arrangement phase she needs to have a good understanding of the different types of arrangement such as:

1. Unison—Unison reading is where most teachers begin. It is unfortunately the most difficult of all arrangements. It is almost impossible to avoid the sing-song monotony which results when inexperienced children read together. Therefore, although one might start with unison reading as a means to help the children feel the rhythm no attempt should be made in the beginning stages to perfect this unison arrangement. Little children particularly may need to start reading in unison. At this time the teacher should work for release so that the children can move. The release and feeling of group participation that unison reading instills acts as a spring board from which to move. When the leader and teacher have had considerable experience unison reading may be very effective. It should not, however, be used exclusively.

2. Antiphonal—The antiphonal arrangement is one of the most enjoyable ways of encouraging children in choral reading. This type of orchestration balances one group of voices with another. There are an infinite number of balancing possibilities. The boys' voices may be balanced with the girls'; a solo voice balanced with a rhythmic chorus; a girl's solo voice balanced with a boy's solo voice with a chorus of girls' and boys' voices in the refrain. The children and the teacher may plan the balance according to the ability and voice quality of the participants. Such antiphonal arrangements may be developed with the children by the trial and error discussion method. Simplicity should be encouraged in the beginning. A poem such as "Wishes" by Rose Fyleman may be a good one for young children. This poem has meaning for them. They have all wished and this poem provides opportunity for a great deal of fun as they work out their antiphonal arrangement.

3. Series of Single Voices—This arrangement may be particularly effective when followed by a group refrain. The poem "Geography" by Eleanor Farjeon lends itself to a variety of single voices of different contrast and quality. Older elementary children may find this poem so arranged a challenge to their imaginations. They may suggest interesting changes after they have tried the single voices and the chorus. It is worth the time and patience necessary to have the children interested in such experimentation.

4. Cumulative arrangement—This is used when the poem calls for a "building to a climax" effect. It is the crescendo arrangement in choral reading. The group may be divided into such groups whose

voices gradually build, one topping the other until a climax has been reached. Young children may enjoy using this cumulative arrangement with a poem such as "Trains" by James Tippett. Variety in this cumulative effect should be encouraged. There are many ways to build a choral reading to a crescendo.

5. Deletion—This is the arrangement where the voices gradually move away from the climax to the conclusion. It is similar to the diminuendo effect in a musical rendition. The example suggested above, "Trains," is suitable for this type of arrangement. The arrangement of the voices gradually moving away may give the effect of the noise of the train gradually dying away in the distance. Such an orchestration demands a real understanding and appreciation of the content of the poem.

6. Three Levels of Voices—This type of arrangement is particularly effective for choral reading with Junior High School children. The difference in the heavy quality of the boys' voices can be used to good advantage. The lightness of the girls' voices contrasts well with the changing voices of the boys. "The Night Wind" by Eugene Field is a good example. The eerie mood and rhythm of the poem lends itself to the arrangement with three levels of voices.

A variety of arrangements are possible with every poem. The arrangement depends upon the response the poem calls forth in the group. Groups vary as do the individuals which make up the group. This creative phase of choral reading calls for concentrated group effort. The results may be spoken music arranged and rendered by an enthusiastic choir.

A teacher can use the dramatic process to help her children enjoy and profit from choral reading. The whole experience may come to life if she coordinates the choral speaking with the dramatic process. The following example may serve to illustrate how a knowledge of the dramatic process and its imaginative utilization in choral speaking made poetry come alive for an entire school.

A teacher who had been brought up in a seaside town moved inland to the prairie. He was homesick for the sea and expressed his feeling by reading aloud "Sea Fever" by John Masefield. Most of the children had never seen the sea or felt the salt air. They had seen the sea on television, but they had not understood their teacher's feeling for the sea until he read the poem. They asked him to read it again. Then one child said softly, "I must go down to the sea. Let's use that poem for our choral speaking. I think I could get into that poem." The class members agreed and the decision to present "Sea Fever" at an assembly program was made.

The teacher used the dramatic process as he guided the children in their preparation of a choral rendition of "Sea Fever." His first objective was to have the children experience the rhythm and tempo of the poetry. To begin, the teacher had the children listen (sense awareness) to a recording of the sounds of the sea. Following this the teacher, who played exceedingly well, improvised the sounds of the sea on the piano. First, the children listened and then the teacher asked them to respond to the music through improvised physical activity (movement). Led by the sound of the rhythm and tempo of the sea the children formed into small groups and became (characterization) the waves, the wind, the rain, and the storm and the calm of the sea. As the music changed its rhythm and tempo, the children changed their movement as they vicariously experienced the sea in a variety of moods. They expressed the movement of the sea in the distance as the wanderer came toward the shore. They felt its rhythm and tempo as they went away from the shore. Adding humming sounds to the movement they improvised relationships between waves, sand, rocks, gulls, and a storm.

Following these active movement expressions the children discussed the human feelings for the sea. They tried to picture what type of person might have written this poem (characterization). *Why* was he lonely for the sea? Would returning to the sea help him? *What* would he find? The teacher suggested that they divide into groups of three or four and decide *who* might have written the poem, *when* he wrote it, and *why*. Each group later prepared a brief improvisation showing their ideas. Many different ideas were presented. The poet, one group decided, was an old man who had run away to sea when he was a boy. He was in a hospital now and he wanted to return to his ocean home and sail out to sea. Another group decided that the poet was a girl whose fiancé had been lost at sea. She wanted to return to her old home and find peace.

After the children improvised the scenes, the teacher told them about the actual poet, John Masefield. At fourteen he was indentured to a merchant ship and became a sea wanderer for several years. He worked at a variety of jobs all over the world but he never forgot the sea. Many of his famous poems told of his love and longing for the sea. In his youth he was considered to be a rough and passionate man who worked always for the masses. Although some of his early work was considered crude, he was finally appointed to the highest rank an English poet can attain. He was made Poet Laureate.

Dramatization of scenes from the poet's life, both imagined and real, were played. A scene on board ship with the young poet as a servant was particularly exciting. John Masefield became a living character to the children. They began to read and enjoy other poems he had written.

The teacher's second objective was to have the children understand the color and quality of the voices they must use to express the underlying feeling of "Sea Fever." Together they discussed what was meant by color and quality in voice. They read the poem silently and picked out the phrases that for them had color and meaning. "The lonely sea and the sky," "gray dawn breaking the flung spray," and "the wind's like a whetted knife," were suggested. Then the teacher divided the class into groups and had them use their voices to express these phrases in a variety of moods—fear, joy, anger, and excitement. The children began to realize that there are several ways of expressing the same phrase. "Gray dawn breaking" when expressed in a mood of fear had quite a different quality from the same phrase expressed in anger.

Again they read the poem to themselves and then in small groups they read the poem in unison. Prior to each reading they decided what the color and quality of the voices would be. One group recited the poem with an excitement of being there. Another decided that the poem was to express longing and another defiance. Each reading was different. A recording of the reading of each group was made and evaluated by the class. The need for clear enunciation and similar pronunciation became apparent. The inflection, the pitch levels, emphasis, and intensity were discussed. The children worked in small groups and in the total group experimented with contrasting pitch levels. They finally came to a conclusion concerning where the emphasis should be placed as they explored the poem's intensity from very soft to very loud. The color and quality expressed by their voices gave the poem a new meaning.

The teacher's final objective was to choose the best structural arrangement. Again the children were divided into groups. One group decided to read the poem using a series of single voices, another preferred a cumulative arrangement, and the third group utilized a three level of voices pattern. Again they played out some characterizations, listened to each other, and devised some meaningful movement patterns. Soon the children were ready for their choral presentation.

The final choral reading of "Sea Fever" was given at a school assembly. It was presented by the three groups in three different ways. Sound effects and music for each reading were supplied by the teacher improvising on the piano. The whole school appeared to enjoy the program.

"I thought choral speaking was always in unison," one teacher commented. "I've never used it because it seemed dull. This, I liked."

"Can we do some 'poetry singing' too?" asked a primary child.

"That was neat-o!" exclaimed a rough and tough third grader.

The teacher was pleased with the result. He had used choral speaking both as a means to an end (appreciation of poetry through sense awareness, movement, and dramatic activities) and as an end in itself (the presentation of an assembly program).

The Dramatic Process and Development of Children's Poetry and Prose

The dramatic process in this publication deals almost exclusively with oral and physical expression. By the time children have reached the intermediate grades, however, they spend an increased amount of their school time in written expression. Meaningful written expression grows most readily from oral expression, and therefore it is appropriate to link the dramatic process and the development of written expression.

Children have a wealth of ideas to express. According to Alastair Reid (p. 104), "Children are interested in anything except, possibly, the things they are expected to be interested in; and we might as well lay our world open to them and let them make off with whatever improbable treasure they discover for themselves." Dramatic activities help children "discover" and " make off" with improbable treasure. These treasures may be experienced and expressed in written form. Suggestions presented to aid in the stimulation of this expression may prove valuable to the elementary teacher.

Drama Ideas and Poetry. Writing poetry is an activity suggested in almost all language arts text books. Exciting and interesting methods of instigating this valuable form of written expression are rare. Kenneth Koch (1971) however, has published a book entitled *Wishes, Lies and Dreams: Teaching Children How to Write Poetry,* which gives some excellent ideas.

"Children," Koch says, "have a natural talent for writing poetry and anyone who teaches them should know that. Teaching really is not the right word for what takes place: it is more like permitting the children to discover something they already have." In drama children are always discovering new personal resources. They express these discoveries in many ways. They become more aware of their sense impressions and their work in art frequently reflects this understanding. They become more aware of the world of movement and their participation in music and dance reflects their understanding of rhythm and tempo. They become more aware of people around them and their understanding of human behavior is reflected in their ability in dramatic characterization, improvisation, and dramatization. Given the opportunity and aided by the dramatic process, children's personal discoveries can also be reflected in writing poetry. Koch believes that poetry is a natural form of expression for children. Frequently their fear of having to spell correctly and of being ridiculed for their poor efforts keeps them from trying to write. They believe poetry is remote and difficult. These are stumbling blocks to producing their own poetry. The solution, he believes, is to treat the children as poets in a nonteacherish way. Get the children happy and excited about the experience of writing poetry and let them use their own ideas is his solution. The following examples of a correlation between the dramatic process and writing poetry is based on the methods suggested by Kenneth Koch in his book.

"I wish" poems are an excellent beginning. Every child knows the meaning of wishes. Having the whole class write a poem together with each child contributing a line beginning with *I wish* can make for a good start. Koch's description of his first assignment with fourth-grade children can set the whole scene for correlation with the dramatic process (Koch 1971,* p. 5).

> Everyone was to write the line on a sheet of paper and turn it in; then I would read them all as a poem. I suggested we make some rules about what should be in every line; this would help to give the final poem unity, and it would help the children to find something to say. I gave an example, putting a color in every line, then asked them for others. We ended up with the regulations that every line should contain a color [what], a comic-strip character [who], and a city or country [where]; also the line should begin with the words, "I wish."

> I collected the lines, shuffled them, and read them aloud as one poem. Some lines obeyed the rules and some didn't; but enough were funny and imaginative to make the whole experience a good one—

> > I wish I was Dick Tracy in a black
> > suit in England
> > I wish that I were a Supergirl with
> > a red cape; the city of Mexico
> > will be where I live
> > I wish that I were Veronica in
> > South America. I wish that
> > I could see the blue sky. . . .

> The children were enormously excited by writing the lines and even more by hearing them read as a poem. They were talking, waving, blushing, laughing, and bouncing up and down. "Feelings at P.S. 61," the title they chose, was not a great poem, but it made them feel like poets and it made them want to write more.

It is interesting to note that Koch's plan was to read the poem to the children. The children would listen (sense awareness) to their creation and thus be able to experience the rhythm and melody. It is also particularly interesting to note that regulations are inherently part of the characterization step in the dramatic process. Every line had to contain color (what), a comic-strip character (who), and a city or country (where).

After the first successful excitement of hearing their "I wish" poem read aloud, I would like to suggest that the children might form into groups of six or seven and try on some different characters, investigate some unusual environments and situations, and then write another poem. One group might write their poem about "animals," another group might choose "adventures," and another group might choose "fears." It is conceivable that some delightful poems might be written. Instead of a color they might choose a substance or a texture. Instead of a comic-strip character they might choose a school or television character, and instead of a city or country they might choose an ocean or a river. Stimulated by active discussion, the trying on of characters and the following of the regulations, the children would experience the feeling of being poets.

Variations on the "I wish" poems are suggested by Koch (1971, p. 7). "Sometimes" and "and" provided a rewarding variation, as shown by the work of fourth grader, Erin Harold.

> Sometimes I wish I had my own
> kitten
> Sometimes I wish I owned a
> puppy
> Sometimes I wish we had a color
> TV
> Sometimes I wish for a room of my
> own
> And I wish all my sisters would
> disappear
> And I wish we didn't have to go
> to school
> And I wish my little sister would
> find her nightgown

And I wish even if she didn't she
   wouldn't wear mine
                —Erin Harold, IV

Such variations give the child a security and a framework without stifling his idea. "I wish" poems are an excellent way to begin poetry. When correlated with the dramatic process and the active sense awareness, movement, and dramatic improvisation it inspires, children become poets.

"Once I understood why the Wish Poems worked so well, I had a much clearer idea of what to look for," writes Kenneth Koch (1971, p. 8).

> A poetry idea should be easy to understand, it should be immediately interesting, and it should bring something new into the children's poems. This could be new subject matter, new sense awareness, new experience of language or poetic form. I looked for other techniques or themes that were, like wishes, a natural and customary part of poetry. I thought of comparisons and then of sounds, and I had the children write a poem about each. As in the Wish Poems, I suggested a repetitive form to help give their poems unity: putting a comparison or a sound in every line. Devoting whole poems to comparisons and sounds gave the children a chance to try out all kinds, and to be as free and as extravagant as they liked. There was no theme or argument with which the sounds or comparisons had to be in accord: they could be experimented with for the pleasures they gave in themselves. In teaching painting an equivalent might be having children paint pictures which were only contrasting stripes or gobs of color.

> In presenting these poetry ideas to the children I encouraged them to take chances. I said people were aware of many resemblances which were beautiful and interesting but which they didn't talk about because they seemed too far- fetched and too silly. But I asked them specifically to look for strange comparisons—if the grass seemed to them like an Easter egg they should say so. I suggested they compare something big to something small, something in school to something out of school, something unreal to something real, something human to something not human. I wanted to rouse them out of the timidity I felt they had about being "crazy" or "silly" in front of an adult in school. There is no danger of children

writing merely nonsensical poems if one does this; the truth they find in freely associating is a greater pleasure to them—

> A breeze is like the sky is coming
>   to you. . . .
>   —Iris Torres, IV

> The sea is like a blue velvet
>   coat.
>   —Argentina Wilkinson, IV

> The flag is as red, white, and blue
>   as the sun's reflection. . . .
>   —Marion Mackles, III

Born of the delight of creating something they had not believed they could, the children are inspired to write. Some prior dramatic games (suggested in primary activities) comparing textures, colors, size, weights, and shapes might precede the writing of comparison poems. The results would hopefully reflect some imaginative feelings. "I wish I lived in a soap bubble made like a crystal ball," was the wish of one fourth-grade child. Add to this line the wish of another: "I wish I had a ray gun like the elephant gun on the wall." (There was a picture in the classroom of an African hunting scene.) Soon the other members of the group stimulated by the funny, the lovely, and the ridiculous would contribute their ideas. They could examine their environment through pictures, films, and books, and by sight, sound, touch and taste, and come up with some excellent poetic expressions. Through movement experiences inspired by comparisons much poetry would evolve. Comparisons of a lyrical nature such as a breeze and a storm, deep blue and russet gold, the fringed leaves and the silvery shine of the boughs, might appear. Strange comparisons such as the "songy sea-weed and jagged mountain peaks," "wind swept roadway and snowmobile trail," "an ache in my throat and a jet stream path," which were suggested by sixth-grade children, might be the beginnings of some unusually expressed individual poems.

Writing a noise poem correlates extremely well with the dramatic process. If the children have had prior experience in playing listening games and making their own tape recordings and becoming attuned to the world of sound, the noise poem is a natural means of poetic expression. If children have not participated in such activities, I suggest that the teacher and the children evolve some listening games together and then write a noise poem. The recording of "sounds I love," "sounds I am afraid of," "noises that laugh," or "noises that squirm" would provide an excellent basis for the writing of a noise poem.

Dream poems also offer a wonderful opportunity to build on the experience of writing wish and noise poems. Movement experiences born of remembered dreams, slow-motion games, absurdities, and listening to recordings played at the wrong speed may help stimulate poetic expression of dream poems.

Another suggestion based on Koch's work adds an idea to help give form to the children's poems. From the suggestion that every odd line begin with "I used to" and every even line with "But now," some very interesting poetry might be created. Using sounds, feelings, fears, likes, and dislikes as a theme both individual and group poems may be written. As a fifth-grade boy who disliked living in a city wrote:

> I used to like the caw of the crow,
> But now the moan of the loon I love.

The final suggestion based on Koch's work challenges the characterization and personification abilities of children. If they have enjoyed using the dramatic process, the "If I were" poems should be a delightful challenge. "Children are so active and so volatile that pretending to be something can be easier for them than describing it," writes Koch.

Because the emphasis in this publication deals with this quality, I suggest that active pretending can lead children to an increased ability for description and thus for the production of poetry. Koch's suggestions for assignments which can stimulate poetry are invaluable for the elementary teacher. Correlating his suggested assignments with drama you too may come to this conclusion (p. 16).

Each assignment gave the children something which they enjoyed writing about and which enabled them to be free and easy and creative. Each also presented them with something new, and thus helped them to have, while they were writing, that feeling of discovery which makes creating works of art so exhilarating.

Drama Ideas and Prose.   Throughout the whole of this publication, ideas for writing have been the suggested result of much of the dramatic activity. It can be noted that children's prose is stimulated by activities involving the dramatic process. A separate section dealing specifically with prose writing seems superfluous. The dramatic process opens much opportunity for prose writing, and the teacher who correlates the previous suggestions on poetry and on speaking and listening will develop her own assignments. Topics for some successful prose assignments correlated with the dramatic process are listed below.

Sense Awareness
    "Sounds of Fear" (or joy, anger, hate, or love)
    "Voices I Love" (or hate, fear, or enjoy)
    "I See as a Giant" (or a mouse, a lion, or a dictator)
    "The Feel of a Volcano" (or a storm, tidal wave, or hurricane)
    "The Taste of Tears" (or laughter or sorrow)
    "The Smell of Horror" (or joy, anger, or delight)

Movement
    "I the Famous Dancer"
    "The Wind and the Rain and Me"
    "A Journey Through Space"

Characterization
    "If I Were King" (or queen, president, or the boss)
    "I Am the Boss"
    "People of the City" (or country or mountains)
    "My Friend the Elephant" (or tiger or witch)
    "Who Are You?"

Improvisation
    "No, We Didn't Do It"
    "Who Says So?"
    "Once Upon a Time There Was a House" (or a school or a church)
    "And Then There Was None"
    "Where Are We?"

Dramatization
    "What Happened?"

"Why?"

"A Stitch in Time Saves Nine" (or any other proverb)

"And Then I Said to the Mayor" (or the general or the principal)

The success of these prose assignments is directly related to their stimulation by discussion and constructive role playing. The structure of the writing improves as the children become aware of the need to make perfectly clear the who, what, where, when, and why of the situation.

The Dramatic Process and the Interpretation of Literature

To be able to interpret the great works of literature so that the experience becomes a personal vivifying of the literary text is one mark of an educated individual. Developing a love for the best literary efforts in the English language is an important educational objective, and to be able to interpret these works for the joy and understanding of oneself and others is an extremely valuable skill.

In the intermediate classroom there is frequently one child who seems to have this ability and he is continually asked to read aloud. "When John reads a story I can see it taking place just like on television," said one fifth-grade child of another. John had developed the ability to interpret the literary works of others so that they became a personalized experience with excitement and significance for himself and those who listened. Young as this child was he had learned through much practice in both silent and oral reading to interpret literature. He had learned the truth of Henri Bergson's (1946, pp. 101–102) statement when he said that if a student is to understand and enjoy a literary text, he will first "have to reinvent it, or in other words, appropriate to a certain extent the inspiration of the author." This reinvention of the literary text is possible for children in elementary schools. It is aided greatly by extensive use of dramatic activities.

In the reinvention of the literary text the interpreter needs to place himself in the situation of the author and the characters he created. He needs to consider how the author and his characters feel, see, hear, and use all their senses. He needs to understand where they live, what they do, and why they do it. He needs to know these characters as real people. For example, before he can interpret Huck Finn, he needs to know *who* Huck Finn is. He must understand something about his background and his relationship with other people. In order to be able to make Huck come alive he needs to try on his colorful speech and make it sound as if he were Huck saying these words. In order to be able to create the environment of the graveyard, he is going to have to imagine the darkness of the night, the sounds of the trees, and all the other atmospheric conditions. "A faint wind moaned through the trees, and Tom feared it might be the spirits of the dead, complaining of being disturbed."[4] Interpreting the *where* takes thought, sensory awareness, and understanding of environment. Interpreting the *what* and *why* of a story also takes some concentrated effort. Reading description and action vividly calls for an understanding of senses, movement, and characterization. The reader must see and feel the action so that the listeners will see it too. The what and the why must come to life as he reads this simple description from *Tom Sawyer*. "Three miles below town the ferry boat stopped at the mouth of a woody hollow and tied up. The crowd swarmed ashore and soon the forest distances and craggy heights echoed far and near with shoutings and laughter. All the different ways of getting hot and tired were gone through with, and by and by the rovers straggled back to camp fortified with responsible appetites, and then the destruction of the good things began."[5]

An understanding of the dramatic process and experience in sensing, moving, and organizing dramatically can be a tremendous aid in interpretation of literature. The listeners will listen to, visualize, and enjoy the reading of children who have become skilled interpreters. Reasonable skill at oral reading and interpretation is possible for most intermediate children. With practice, encouragement, and use of drama, a love of literature and its interpretation can be developed.

---

[4]Mark Twain, *The Adventures of Tom Sawyer.* New York: Grosset and Dunlap, 1946, p. 88.

[5]Twain, p. 244.

The Dramatic Process and Reading Aloud.   Spontaneous activities involving the dramatic process preceding the preparation of a selection of literature for oral interpretation can be of great assistance in reading aloud. Continuing with the example of *Tom Sawyer,* the following suggestions are made.

Good oral reading grows from silent reading; therefore, the need to first read the selection silently is assumed. Following the silent reading of the story, a series of dramatic activities involving the story will help make the reading come alive.

Through activities involving the sense awareness step in the dramatic process an understanding of the times of Tom Sawyer can be gained. Dramatic games involving the sense stimulation of that time are in order. The teacher might begin, "If you were suddenly to find yourself in Hannibal, Missouri, in the 1840's, what would you hear? Close your eyes, blot out the twentieth century and listen. What would you see? What kind of school would you be in? Pick up the items you would find on your desk. Feel them. What kind of implements would you find in front of you? Listen again. What kinds of lessons would you hear? What would you see outside? What would you be wearing? Examine your jacket. The bell rings. What would you do? What games would you play?"

The children may need to go back to the written script in order to find and understand their answers to these questions. However, by such simple activities as these, the children can begin to sense the differences between now and then and between themselves and Tom and Huck.

The movement step in the dramatic process can be used in much the same way. Music from the *Mark Twain Suite* may help carry the children back to a slower, quieter pace. Moving to adverbs found in the silent reading may help set the mood and atmosphere. Such adverbs as elaborately, grotesquely, yearningly, beseechingly, desolately, pleasurably, fidgetingly, inevitably, compellingly, preposterously, murderously, and frighteningly selected by the children and teacher from the book can add to the appreciation of the work.

Opportunities to use the characterization, improvisation, and dramatization steps are numerous. Trying on the characters of

Aunt Polly, Widow Douglas, Injun Joe, Muff Potter, Tom, Huck, Sid, and Becky can be rewarding. Placing these characters in group and individual situations can lead to a deeper understanding of the novel and therefore a more interesting interpretation. Some suggestions to help make the dialogue vivid might be: (1) Tom and Sid discussing the possibilities of the coming Sabbath, (2) Huck and Tom discussing the same situation, (3) Tom and Becky discussing school, (4) Tom and Huck discussing the schoolmaster, (5) Tom and Muff Potter discussing the future, (6) Injun Joe and Huck discussing the law, (7) Dr. Robinson and Tom discussing medicine, (8) the minister and the schoolmaster discussing their pupils, (9) Tom telling Sid about his cave adventures, and (10) Tom, Huck, Becky, Joe Harper, Ben Rogers, and the rest of their classmates talking about their future careers.

Group improvisations and dramatizations entitled: (1) Lost in the Cave, (2) Murder in the Graveyard, (3) Let's Be Pirates, (4) School—1840 Style, and (5) The Trial of Muff Potter would help make the speech and thoughts of the characters vivid and the incidents more readily described. Living the events spontaneously would improve the understandability of future oral interpretation.

There is a great difference between the improvised language of a story and its planned oral interpretation. The former, however, can help to make the latter live. Although it is unwise to let the improvised dramatic activities become the main goal, it is one way of making this current main objective (that of interpreting the works of others) live!

The Dramatic Process and Readers Theater. "Readers Theatre," according to two prominent authorities, "is a medium in which two or more oral interpreters through their oral reading cause an audience to experience literature" (Coger and White 1967, 8). Although it is an art form usually performed by adults, its form can very profitably be adapted for participants of elementary school age. Generally, Readers Theater varies from a conventional play in five specific ways (Coger and White 1967, p. 19):

1. Scenery and costumes are only very selectively used,
2. Action or physical movement is merely suggested by interpretation and is visualized in the minds of the audience,

3. A narrator speaking directly to the audience, usually establishes the basic situation or theme and links the various segments together,
4. A physical script is usually carried by the reader,
5. There is a continuing effort to develop and maintain a closer, more personalized relationship between performer and audience.

Selecting and adapting material for Readers Theater is a very interesting and challenging project for older children. It will, however, take a great deal of help from the teacher. All stories do not adapt themselves well to this form. Effective material must have action and characters of compelling interest, evocative power, vivid language, and wholeness. For preparation by children an added dimension of child interest must be added.

Both prose and poetry can be adapted for children. If a teacher is vitally interested in using this art form, she should read extensively about the selection and adaptation of prose before attempting to adapt material for presentation to other than a classroom audience. For the purposes of this publication, however, all suggestions are made as an aid to helping children love and interpret literature. The children's Readers Theater adaptation of a story for presentation to the rest of the class is the suggested activity. The dramatic process aids greatly in helping the children interpret literature that appeals to them.

A simplified adaptation of an incident from *Tom Sawyer* is presented here as a brief example of how children and teacher could adapt and present a brief incident in a favorite story. The selection is chosen because of the eternal drama of "playing out" literature.

TOM SAWYER
BY MARK TWAIN
ADAPTED FOR READERS THEATER

CAST OF CHARACTERS:
    Narrator
    Tom
    Joe Harper

SCENE: A Wood Near Hannibal, Missouri, in 1845.

NARRATOR: Tom Sawyer entered a dense wood, picked his pathless way to the center of it and sat down on a mossy spot under a spreading oak. The boy's soul was steeped in melancholy; his feelings were in accord with his surroundings. It seemed to him that life was but a trouble, at best, and he more than half envied Jimmy Hodges, so lately released; it must be very peaceful, he thought, to lie and slumber and dream for ever and ever. If he only had a clean Sunday-school record he could be willing to go, and be done with it all. Ah, if he could only die temporarily. But the elastic heart of youth cannot be compressed into one constrained shape long at a time. Tom presently began to drift insensibly back into the concerns of life again.

TOM: What if I went away? Ever so far away. Into unknown countries beyond the seas and never came back any more!

NARRATOR: The idea of being a clown recurred to him now.

TOM: No! I'll be a soldier and return many years from now, all war-worn and illustrious.

NARRATOR: That idea appealed to him for a moment.

TOM: No, better still, I'll join Indians and hunt buffaloes and go on the warpath.

NARRATOR: But, no, there was something gaudier even than that.

TOM: I'll be a *pirate!*

NARRATOR: Now his future lay plain before him and glowing with unimaginable splendor. How his name would fill the world, and make people shudder! How gloriously he would go plowing the dancing seas, in his long, low, black-hulled racer, the "Spirit of the Storm," with his grisly flag flying at the fore! And at the zenith of his fame, how he would suddenly appear at the old village and stalk into church, brown and weather-beaten, in his black velvet doublet and trunks, his great jack boots, his crimson sash, his belt bristling with horse pistols, his crime-rusted cutlass at his side, his slouch hat with waving plumes, his black flag unfurled, with the skull and crossbones on it, and hear with swelling ecstasy the whisperings. . . .

TOM: "It's Tom Sawyer, the Pirate—the Black Avenger of the Spanish Main."

NARRATOR: Yes, it was settled; his career was determined. He would run away from home and enter upon it. He would start the very next morning. Therefore, he must now begin to get ready. He would collect his resources together. He went to a rotten log near at hand and began to dig under one end of it with his barlow knife. He soon struck wood that sounded hollow. He put his hand there and uttered this incantation impressively:

Tom: What hasn't come here, *come!* What's here, *stay* here!

Narrator: Then he scraped away the dirt, and exposed a pine shingle. He took it up and disclosed a shapely little treasure house whose bottom and sides were of shingles. In it lay a marble. Tom's astonishment was boundless! He scratched his head with a perplexed air.

Tom: Well, that beats anything!

Narrator: He tossed the marble away and stood cogitating. The truth was that a superstition of his had failed, here, which he and all his comrades had always looked upon as infallible. If you buried a marble with certain necessary incantations, and left it alone a fortnight, and then opened the place with the incantation he had just used, you would find that all the marbles you had ever lost had gathered themselves together there, meantime, no matter how widely they had been separated. But, now this thing had actually and unquestionably failed. Tom's whole structure of faith was shaken to its foundations. He had many a time heard of this thing succeeding, but never of its failing before. It did not occur to him that he had tried it several times before, himself, but could never find the hiding places afterward. He puzzled over the matter some time, and finally decided that some witch had interfered and broken the charm. He thought he would satisfy himself on that point; so he searched around till he found a small sandy spot with a little funnel-shaped depression in it. He laid himself down and put his mouth close to this depression and called:

Tom: Doodlebug, doodlebug, tell me what I want to know!
Doodlebug, doodlebug, tell me what I want to know!

Narrator: The sand began to work, and suddenly a small black bug appeared for a second, then darted away.

Tom: He dasn't tell! So it *was* a witch that done it. I just knowed it.

NARRATOR:	Just here the blast of a toy tin trumpet came faintly down the green aisles of the forest. Tom flung off his jacket and trousers, turned a suspender into a belt, raked away some brush behind the rotten log, disclosing a rude bow and arrow, a lath sword and a tin trumpet, and in a moment had seized these things and bounded away, barelegged, with fluttering shirt. He presently halted under a great elm, blew an answering blast, and then began to tiptoe and look warily out, this way and that. He said cautiously—to an imaginary company:
TOM:	Hold, my merry men! Keep hid till I blow.
NARRATOR:	Now Joe Harper appeared, clad and armed as Tom.
TOM:	Hold! Who comes here into Sherwood Forest without my pass?
JOE:	Guy of Guisborne wants no man's pass. Who art thou that—that—
TOM:	Dares to hold such language.
NARRATOR:	Said Tom, for they talked by the book from memory.
JOE:	Who art thou that dares to hold such language?
TOM:	I, indeed! I am Robin Hood, as thy caitiff carcass soon shall know.
JOE:	Then art thou indeed that famous outlaw? Right gladly will I dispute with thee the passes of the merry wood. Have at thee!
NARRATOR:	They took their lath swords, dumped their other traps on the ground, struck a fencing attitude, foot to foot, and began a grave, careful combat, "two up and two down."
TOM:	Now, if you've got the hang, go it lively!
NARRATOR:	So they "went it lively," panting and perspiring with the work. By and by Tom shouted:
TOM:	Fall! Fall! Why don't you fall?
JOE:	I shan't! Why don't you fall yourself? You're getting the worst of it.
TOM:	Why, that ain't anything. *I* can't fall; that ain't the way it is in the book. The book says, "Then with one back-handed stroke he slew poor Guy of Guisborne." You're to turn around and let me hit you in the back.
NARRATOR:	There was no getting around the authorities, so Joe turned, received the whack, and fell.
JOE:	Now [getting up], you got to let me kill *you.* That's fair.

TOM:	Why, I can't do that, it ain't in the book.
JOE:	Well, it's blamed mean—that's all.
TOM:	Well, say, Joe, you can be Friar Tuck or Much the miller's son, and lam me with a quarterstaff; or I'll be the Sheriff of Nottingham and you be Robin Hood a little while and kill me.
NARRATOR:	This was satisfactory, and so these adventures were carried out. Then Tom became Robin Hood again, and was allowed by the treacherous nun to bleed his strength away through his neglected wound. And at last Joe, representing a whole tribe of weeping out-laws, dragged him sadly forth, gave his bow into his feeble hands, and Tom said:
TOM:	Where this arrow falls, there bury poor Robin Hood under the greenwood tree.
NARRATOR:	Then he shot the arrow and fell back and would have died, but he lit on a nettle and sprang up too gaily for a corpse. The boys dragged themselves, hid their accouterments, and went off grieving that there were no outlaws any more, and wondering what modern civilization could claim to have done to com-pensate for their loss. They said they would rather be outlaws a year in Sherwood Forest than President of the United States forever.

There are many other favorite stories which might be so adapted. Sixth-grade children might find the selection, adaptation, preparation, and presentation of Readers Theater a challenge and focus for the understanding of literature. Although this form of oral interpretation is generally accepted as an adult activity, its challenge for use with older children is great.

DEVELOPMENT OF PROBLEM SOLVING SKILLS

Life is a series of problem solving crises. Adults are continually called upon to solve problems. The problem of course selection looms large in the life of a college student. Problems of money and its management are ever present in the lives of businessmen and housewives. Problems involving justice and the law weigh heavily upon lawyers and public servants. Children also face problem situations. These are problems that are as large and difficult for the child as are the problems that face adults. Problems involving the use of time (school work versus television viewing), problems involving honesty (punishment versus no punishment), and problems involving joining the gang (peer acceptance versus adult authority) are very real and must be faced by every child in intermediate grades. The attitude one has toward problems and the methods one uses to solve these ever present big and small crises are developed in childhood. The child who learns to face problem solving situations constructively and creatively is fortunate. The methods he uses to help in their solution are frequently learned in elementary school.

During the past twenty years there has been an increasing emphasis placed upon the development of creative problem solving skills. Leaders in business and industry have initiated creative problem solving programs for engineers and management personnel (Davis and Scott 1971, pp. 58–105). E. Paul Torrance, prominent leader in educational research, has conducted a series of Teacher Workshops, one of which deals with creative problem solving skills. With a colleague he has developed a group of elementary creativity programs (Myers and Torrance 1964, 1965, 1966a, 1966b, 1966c) which include many problem solving activities and utilize many of the elements in the dramatic process.

The creative problem solving skills workshop initiated by Torrance uses the approach formulated by Alex Osborn whose interest in creativity led to the establishment of the Creative Education Foundation in 1954. Osborn (Parnes and Harding 1962, pp. 19–29) writes that the creative problem solving process is comprised of the following procedures.

1. *Fact finding*, which includes problem definition (picking out and pointing up the problem) and preparation (gathering and analyzing the pertinent data).
2. *Idea finding*, which includes idea production (thinking up tentative ideas as possible leads) and idea development (selecting from resultant ideas, adding others, and reprocessing by means of modification and combination).
3. *Solution finding*, which includes verifying the tentative solutions and adoption.

This creative problem solving process correlates well with the dramatic process as discussed in this publication. Using an extended example I will trace this correlation to illustrate how drama may help to develop the problem solving skills of elementary school children.

The children referred to in this example were members of a sixth grade in a large inner city area. They were a year or two older than most sixth graders and they were bored with school in general and language arts in particular. At the time this incident began the whole school was in a state of upheaval over security problems. There was much vandalism and stealing. The policemen in the area were under constant strain as were the teachers and children. The biggest problems facing the entire school concerned the students' relationship with and attitude toward the law.

A new teacher joined the staff at this time to replace one who had resigned in fear for his personal safety. The newcomer, a former student in the school, had had some experience with drama and role-playing. He believed he had an understanding of some of the problems involved, so he decided to conduct a drama workshop which would zero in on police and student problems. His method of approach and what happened as he and the children became involved shows a correlation between the Osborn problem solving process and the dramatic process.

The Dramatic Process and Fact Finding

The new teacher began his first class by showing the children a large photograph. It was a picture of a uniformed policeman phoning from a glass enclosed telephone booth. The booth was situated on a busy street corner. A few run-down buildings were visible as was a large overturned rubbish can and some broken glass. The man's back was turned away from the camera and he was lounging as he talked into the phone. Immediately the picture brought forth some rather harsh comments. The teacher listened and began asking the following questions.

"Who is this man?"

"What does he do on his day off?"

"What kind of a community does he live in?"

"Does he have a family?"

"Who is he phoning?"

"Did he instigate the call?"

"What type of community does he work in?"

"What duties does he perform?"

"Does he have any problems?"

"What is his main problem?"

"How do you know it is a problem?"

The teacher did not comment. He asked the questions and waited to hear a variety of sometimes sarcastic and even crude answers. He waited until every child who appeared to want to contribute an idea had had a chance to do so. Gradually, the comments became less emotional and more specific. By the time the teacher began asking about the problems the children appeared to be responding quite reasonably.

"Now," said the teacher, "I am going to ask the same questions again. This time, however, you must back up your comments with observable facts. My first question is: "Who is this man?"

"He's a cop," called out one of the boys.

"How do you know? What facts do you have to support your idea?" the teacher asked.

"He's in a cop's uniform," replied the boy.

"Yeah, and he is phoning headquarters," added another.

"Headquarters?" questioned the teacher. "Why do you believe that?"

"That's what they always do. They squeal to headquarters," was the explanation.

"You mean that every phone call made is made to police headquarters?" asked the teacher.

"No, but . . . ," admitted the child.

"You'll have to have evidence for that statement. He may be phoning headquarters, but that isn't a known fact."

"Well, he's a white policeman in a black area," began another child.

"What facts do you have to support that?" asked the teacher.

"I can see he is white and all that junk shows that it's a black area," was the reply.

"Is that a fact?" commented the teacher. "I can see there is junk around, but that doesn't make it a black area. I've seen lots of junk in many white areas too. You'll have to produce the facts."

The discussion became quite lively as the children found facts to support their comments. By the time they had discussed all the questions, facts were beginning to be separated from fancy. They also decided that maybe the policeman had some problems they'd never considered.

"What would you say was the main problem a policeman would have in this area?" asked the teacher.

After considerable disagreement and discussion they finally agreed on one specific problem. "Knowing who he could trust," was their final conclusion.

This showed unusual understanding. The idea that policemen might have problems hadn't occurred to these children. Through discussion with emphasis on fact finding the children had begun to think about being in someone else's shoes. They had begun to realize that facts are needed to support observations before problems can be defined. This use of the first step in the dramatic process (sense awareness) led naturally to another step (characterization) and to the heart of the process—role enactment. Once the children in this sixth-grade class had defined the problem which emerged from the observation of a picture and gathered the pertinent data available, they were ready to proceed to the next procedure in problem solving.

The Dramatic Process and Idea Finding

One of the basic concepts of creative problem solving is that quantity breeds quality, particularly when accompanied by deferred judgement. Scientific research has shown that when it comes to idea formation those who think up twice as many ideas think up more than twice as many good ideas in the same length of time (Parnes and Harding 1962, p. 21). Therefore in this idea finding procedure the teacher needs to encourage the children to give as many ideas as possible and defer his judgement concerning them.

Stating the problem simply the teacher began the discussion. "You believe that the policeman's biggest problem is knowing who to trust. How can he find out?"

"He can ask questions."

"He can watch how the guys talk to other guys."

"He can look at their friends."

"He could bug the guy and see what he does."

"He could ask someone to squeal on the guy."

"How about asking the teacher?"

"How about listening when kids are having a bash?"

"He could look up his record at the station."

"Frisk him."

The ideas suggested were simple and within the children's experience. They all appeared interested in considering the ideas so the teacher decided to try some role playing activity. In this way he expected that the children would select, modify, and combine their ideas in preparation for a meaningful solution.

"Let's divide into pairs," said the teacher. "One be the policeman and the other be the kid he wants to trust. Now, as policemen, use your ideas and see if he is trustworthy."

Immediately the classroom became alive with talking. Working together in pairs the children were totally involved. As the teacher observed the group, he began to pick out different characters. He noted some rough handling by the "policemen" and some sly maneuvering by the "kids." He also saw some frisking and fighting by both policemen and kids. The majority of the group, however, were involved in discussion about the situation and playing out their ideas.

Following this role playing experience, the teacher held a group discussion. "What ideas worked?" he asked the children. "How can a policeman learn to trust? What did you policemen learn?"

"I looked him straight in the eye and asked him questions. I trusted him by the look in his eye."

"It's the questions you ask that counts. I asked the kid questions I knew the answers to. When he gave me the wrong answers I knew I couldn't trust him."

"Can you explain what you mean?" asked the teacher. Soon the answers developed into a detailed discussion on the concept of trust. This led to two group improvisations, one involving a gang of kids a policeman couldn't trust, and the other a gang of kids a policeman could trust. The improvisations played out showed clearly some of the reasons why the children and police mistrusted each other.

The first improvisation involved a gang of kids hanging around a street corner. An argument began, a fight started, and a stabbing occurred. As the members of the gang tried to shield the attacker and aid the attacked, a policeman rushed up shouting, "I'll get you kids for this! Who did it? You can't get away with it this time. Where is the knife?" As the policeman frisked the children, the weapon was passed slyly from one to the other. Frustrated and angry at not finding the knife, the policeman shouted for help. At this moment two of the boys jumped at him and threw him to the ground, and the gang scattered. The scene ended with the policeman trying to explain to his friends why he had called for help when no gang could be seen.

The second improvisation involved a gang of kids playing baseball on a field. Almost immediately a ball went over a fence and crashed into a store front window. Out rushed the angry shopkeeper shouting, "You young hoodlums. I'll get you for this. You did it on purpose!" At this point the policeman who trusted the children arrived on the scene and tried to calm the irate man. He called the gang together, asked questions, got the truthful answers, and convinced the shopkeeper that it had been an accident. The scene ended with the shopkeeper admitting that since it was an accident his insurance company would pay for the damage.

The two improvisations were very interesting and showed the result of some of their fact and idea finding procedures. There was a decided change in their attitude toward policemen. The chief difference now lay in the fact that the children were looking at the policeman's side of the situation as well as their own. They had proceeded from talking about a series of complaints against the law to participating in an improvisation that demanded trust. These children whose lives were full of mistrust were beginning to see that there might be another side to the law. They had selected ideas, modified, and combined them with others, then with the help of the dramatic process they were ready to experiment with a solution.

The Dramatic Process and Solution Finding

At this point the teacher returned to the picture he had shown the children the first day. Now the children decided to do a dramatization based on the picture. Their new ideas and insights showed as they discussed their plan of approach.

"Let's look carefully at the picture again," the teacher began. "We must decide exactly who is this man?"

"He is a new guy on our beat."

"He is friendly and wants us to like him."

"But we don't," interjected one of the boys. "He's a cop."

"I think he is one we can trust."

"No, I don't want to play it that way. I don't trust him," insisted the young man.

"Let's play the guy the way we want to. When you are the policeman, he can be a skunk. When I play him, he is going to be just dumb," decided the other boy.

The teacher continued aiding with questions. "Who is the man phoning? Why? What duties are assigned to him? What happened five minutes before the picture was taken? What will happen when he hangs up the receiver?" As the children organized their answers, the teacher noted which ones were practical and which ones received general consensus. Finally, he summed up their ideas to be dramatized in the following manner.

"You see here in the picture a white policeman who has just begun his career. He is a fine strong young man, but he is not too bright. He is phoning to the police station to report that all is fine. He is trying to make friends, but, outside the booth, two boys are waiting to get him. They are after him for arresting them last week. What is going to happen? Who wants to play the policeman? Who will play the waiting boys?"

There were several willing candidates for the attackers and a few for the policeman. Finally, three were chosen and a brief scene was played. After the evaluation-discussion the scene was enlarged to include other children and characters on the street corner. With each replaying the dramatization was expanded and the characters and ideas were modified. The conclusion for the dramatization was played in several different ways. Additional problems evolved including an arrest and a get away. One playing included a shop-lifting problem where children alternately took the roles of offender, store manager, and arresting officer.

In this manner the children participated in the third procedure of the creative problem solving process. They attempted to verify tentative solutions by playing out (dramatization) trust situations. The main problem of developing trust between children and policemen was continually discussed as they evaluated their efforts.

A solution was finally arrived at. From their playing out of a variety of incidents the leader of the group explained the solution. "If the cop trusts you, you trust him. You can tell by feeling when he does." This appeared to sum up their solution for the problem of trust. Their adoption of the solution in their lives was a different matter. Problems continued to exist in the school. However, both the teacher and the children had learned from this problem solving experience. They had for at least a short time placed themselves in someone else's shoes. This central aspect in the dramatic process had added to their understanding and problem solving potential.

CONCLUSION

The language arts form the backbone of the elementary school curriculum. Listening, speaking, reading, and writing are vital skills, which must be mastered in the early years if advanced learning is to take place. Imaginative use of the dramatic process in the developing of these skills can help make language learning live. Try it.

REFERENCES

BARNES, DOUGLAS. *Drama in the English Classroom.* Urbana, Ill.: National Council of Teachers of English, 1968.

*BARTON, ROBERT; BOOTH, DAVID; BUCKLES, AGNES; AND MOORE, WILLIAM. *Nobody in the Cast.* Don Mills, Ontario: Longman's of Canada, 1969.

BERGSON, HENRI L. *The Creative Mind.* Westport, Conn.: Greenwood Inc., 1946.

*BOORMAN, JOYCE. *Creative Dance in Grades Four to Six.* Don Mills, Ontario: Longman's of Canada, 1971.

*_____. *Creative Dance in the First Three Grades.* New York: David McKay Co., Inc., 1969.

*BURTON, E. J. *Teaching English Through Self Expression.* London: Evans, 1949.

CARLTON, LESSIE, AND MOORE, ROBERT H. *Reading, Self-Directive Dramatizations and Self Concept.* Columbus, Ohio: Charles E. Merrill Publishing Co., 1968.

COGER, IRENE L., AND WHITE, MELVIN R. *Readers Theatre Handbook: A Dramatic Approach to Literature.* Glenview, Ill.: Scott, Foresman and Company, 1967.

DAVIS, GARY A., AND SCOTT, JOSEPH A., Eds. *Training Creative Thinking.* New York: Holt, Rinehart & Winston, Inc., 1971.

EDUCATION SURVEY 2. *Drama.* London: Department of Education and Science, Her Majesty's Stationery Office, 1967.

GALVIN, KATHLEEN M., AND BOOK, CASSANDRA L. *Special Communication: An Interpersonal Approach for Teachers.* Skokie, Ill.: National Textbook, 1972.

GULLAN, MARJORIE. *Choral Speaking.* London: Methuen and Company, 1931.

HANSEN, BRIAN, AND CONTRUCCI, JUDIE. *Theatre Game File.* St. Louis: Aesthetic Education Program of CEMREL, Inc., 1971.

HAYES, ELOISE. *Language Change and Creative Drama.* Classroom Practices in Teaching English—1968–69. Urbana, Ill.: National Council of Teachers of English, 1970.

HEATHCOTE, DOROTHY. "Improvisation." *English in Education.* London: The Bodley Head Ltd., Autumn 1967.

IRWIN, ELEANOR C. "The Effect of a Program of Creative Dramatics upon Personality as Measured by the California Test of Personality, Sociograms, Teacher's Ratings, and Grades." Ph.D. dissertation, University of Pittsburgh, 1963.

---

*Recommended readings and research to aid in the further study of drama and drama education.

Kemp, David. A Different Drummer, An Ideas Book for Drama. Toronto, Ontario: McClelland and Stewart, Limited, 1972.

Koch, Kenneth. *Wishes, Lies and Dreams: Teaching Children to Write Poetry.* New York: Random House, Inc., 1971.

Laban, Rudolf. *Modern Educational Dance.* London: MacDonald and Evans, Ltd., 1968.

Linn, John et al. Language Patterns. Language Arts Series. Toronto: Holt, Rinehart & Winston of Canada, 1968.

Ludwig, Charlotte. "The Effects of Creative Dramatics Activities upon the Articulation Skills of Kindergarten Children." Master's thesis, University of Pittsburgh, 1955.

May, Frank B. Teaching Language as Communication to Children. Columbus, Ohio: Charles E. Merrill Publishing Co., 1967.

McCaslin, Nellie. Creative Dramatics in the Classroom. New York: David McKay Co., Inc., 1968.

McIntyre, Barbara. *The Art of Teaching Choral Reading—A Report of the Twenty-first Annual Conference on Reading.* Pittsburgh: University of Pittsburgh, 1965.

_____. *Creative Dramatics Elementary School Language Arts: Selected Readings.* Chicago: Rand McNally & Co., 1969.

_____. "The Effect of Creative Activities on the Articulation Skills of Children." *Speech Monographs.* March 1958.

Moffet, James. A Student-Centered Language Arts Curriculum, Grades K–13: A Handbook for Teachers. Boston: Houghton Mifflin Company, 1968.

Myers, R. E., and Torrance, Paul. *Can You Imagine?* Boston: Ginn & Co., 1966a.

_____. *For Those Who Wonder.* Boston: Ginn & Co., 1966b.

_____. *Invitation to Speaking and Writing Creatively.* Boston: Ginn & Co., 1965.

_____. *Invitation to Thinking and Doing.* Boston: Ginn & Co., 1964.

_____. *Plots, Puzzles, and Plays.* Boston: Ginn & Co., 1966c.

Parnes, Sidney J., and Harding, Harold P., Eds. *A Source Book for Creative Thinking.* New York: Charles Scribner's & Sons, 1962.

Piaget, Jean. *The Construction of Reality in the Child.* New York: Ballantine, 1971.

Quig, James. "Book Early—How to Get Young Children Excited About Reading." *Week-End Magazine, Victoria Times.* May 5, 1973.

Rakin, Paul T. "The Importance of Listening Ability," *Clearing House* 30 (October 1955): pp. 103–106.

Reid, Alastair. "A Poet's View of Childhood." *The Atlantic Monthly* (March 1963).

*Russell, Joan. *Creative Dance in the Primary School.* New York: Frederick A. Praeger Inc., 1968.

*Siks, Geraldine. *Creative Dramatics: An Art for Children.* New York: Harper Brothers, 1958.

*Smith, James A. *Creative Teaching of Language Arts in the Elementary School.* Boston: Allyn & Bacon, Inc., 1967.

*Spolin, Viola. *Improvisation for the Theatre.* Evanston, Ill.: Northwestern University Press, 1963.

Tucker, Jo Anne Klineman. "The Use of Creative Dramatics as an Aid in Developed Reading Readiness with Kindergarten Children." Ph.D. dissertation, University of Wisconsin, 1971.

Valett, Robert E. *The Remediation of Learning Disabilities.* Belmont, Calif.: Feron Publishers, 1967.

*Wagner, Jeanine, and Baker, Kitty. *A Place for Ideas—Our Theatre.* San Antonio, Texas: Principia Press of Trinity University Press, 1965.

*Ward, Winifred. *Playmaking with Children.* New York: Appleton-Century Crofts, 1957.

_____. *Stories to Dramatize.* Anchorage, Ky.: Anchorage Press, 1952.

*Way, Brian. *Development Through Drama.* New York: Humanities Press, 1967.

AUDIO-VISUAL MATERIALS

Films

**Discovery and Experience: Movement in Time and Space.* B.B.C.T.V. Enterprises, London.

**Learning Through Movement.* S-L Film Productions, Los Angeles, California.

**Omnibus: Three Looms Waiting.* B.B.C.T.V. Enterprises, London.

Records

**Count Down for Listening, Speech Improvement Series of Twenty-Four Lessons for Intermediate Grades.* Educational Activities, Inc., Freeport, N.Y., 1969.

Dance A Story Series, RCA Victor.

**Listening with Mr. Bunny Big Ears, Language Development and Speech Improvement Through Dramatic Play for Primary Age Children: A Series of Twenty-Four Lessons.* Educational Activities, Freeport, N.Y. 1965.

Name Index

Subject Index

THE BOOK MANUFACTURE

CREATIVE DRAMA IN THE ELEMENTARY SCHOOL was composed in computerized typography at Datagraphics in Phoenix. Printing and binding were by George Banta Company, Inc., Menasha, Wisconsin. Internal design was by F. E. Peacock Publishers, Inc. art depart - ment. Cover design was by Charles Kling & Associates.